Mary:
Jesus' Mother—
and Ours

A Guided Discovery for Groups and Individuals

Kevin Perrotta

LOYOLA PRESS.
A JESUIT MINISTRY
Chicago

LOYOLA PRESS.
A JESUIT MINISTRY

3441 N. Ashland Avenue
Chicago, Illinois 60657
(800) 621-1008
www.loyolapress.com

In accordance with c. 827, permission to publish is granted on July 29, 2011 by Rev. Msgr. John F. Canary, Vicar General of the Archdiocese of Chicago. Permission to publish is an official declaration of ecclesiastical authority that the material is free from doctrinal and moral error. No legal responsibility is assumed by the grant of this permission.

Unless otherwise noted, the Scripture quotations contained herein are from the New Revised Standard Version Bible: Catholic Edition, copyright © 1993 and 1989 by the Division of Christian Education of the National Council of the Churches of Christ in the U.S.A. Used by permission. All rights reserved. Subheadings in Scripture quotations have been added by Kevin Perrotta.

Excerpts from the English translation of *The Roman Missal* © 2010, International Commission on English in the Liturgy Corporation. All rights reserved. Used with permission.

Interior design by Kay Hartmann/Communique Design
Illustration by Anni Betts

ISBN–13: 978-0-8294-3536-8; ISBN–10: 0-8294-3536-0

Printed in the United States of America
16 17 18 Bang 10 9 8 7 6 5 4 3 2

Contents

How to Use This Guide

Our approach in this book is *guided discovery*. It is *guided* because we all need support in understanding Scripture and in reflecting on what it means for our lives. Scripture was written to be understood and applied within the community of faith. We read the Bible *for* ourselves but not *by* ourselves. Whether we are reading in a group or on our own, we need resources that aid us in understanding. Our approach is also one of *discovery,* because all of us need to encounter Scripture for ourselves and consider its meaning to our life. No one can do this for us.

This book is designed to give you both guidance for understanding and tools for discovery. You can use it in a group or alone.

The introduction provides some background and helps orient you for our exploration of the life of Mary, the mother of Jesus, in the Gospels. Then, each week, the "Exploring the Theme" section, after the Gospel readings, will help bring out their meaning. Supplementary material at the end of most sessions offers further resources for understanding and reflection.

The main tool for discovery in this guide is the "Questions for Reflection and Discussion" section in each session. The first questions in the section will spur you to notice things in the text, to sharpen your powers of observation, and to read for comprehension. The remaining questions suggest ways to compare the people, situations, and experiences in the biblical texts with your own life and the world today—an important step toward grasping what God is saying to *you* through the Scripture and what your response should be. Choose the questions that you think will work best for you and your group. It is highly recommended that you prepare to answer all the questions before your group meets.

It is a good idea to pay particular attention to the final question each week, labeled "Focus Question." This question points to an especially important issue that the reading raises. You may find it difficult to answer the focus question in brief. Make sure to leave enough time for everyone in the group to discuss it!

Other sections encourage you to take an active approach to your Bible reading and discussion. At the start of each session, "Questions to Begin" will help you break the ice and get the conversation flowing. These questions are usually light and have only a slight connection to the reading. After each Scripture reading, there is an opportunity for each person in the group to offer a brief "first impression." This is a chance to express an initial, personal response to the text. Each session ends with the "Prayer to Close," which suggests a way of expressing your response to God.

How long are the discussion sessions? We've assumed that you will have about an hour and twenty minutes for discussions. If you have less time, you'll find that you can shorten most of the elements somewhat.

Is homework necessary? You will get the most out of your discussions if you read the weekly material and prepare your answers to the questions in advance of each meeting. If participants are not able to prepare, then you can read the "Exploring the Theme" sections aloud at the points where they appear.

What about leadership? You don't have to be an expert in the Bible to lead a discussion. Choose one or two people to act as discussion facilitators, and have everyone in the group read "Suggestions for Bible Discussion Groups" (pages 92–94) before beginning.

Does everyone need a guide? A Bible? Everyone in the group will need his or her own copy of this book. It contains the biblical texts for reflection and discussion, so a Bible is not absolutely necessary—but each person will find it useful to have one. You should have at least one Bible on hand for your discussions. (See page 96 for recommendations.)

Before you begin, take a look at the suggestions for Bible discussion groups (pages 92–94) or individuals (page 95).

Mary in Her Place and Time

After centuries of employing patriarchs, prophets, kings, and sages in his saving plan for humanity, God reached the point at which he needed an extraordinarily humble and reliable person to carry out a crucial mission. For this task he chose someone who, in today's world, might not be old enough to get a driver's permit and certainly wouldn't be allowed to travel to World Youth Day without a chaperone. We are talking, of course, about Mary of Nazareth.

What is remarkable about Mary at first sight is how unremarkable she was. When God called her, the length and breadth of her life experience was, well, not very long or wide. She lived in a flyspeck village and may have been as young as thirteen years old. She was poor, and her family so insignificant that the Gospel writers don't even mention them. No one was more surprised than Mary that God called her to a great work. "He has looked with favor on the lowliness of his servant," she marveled, referring to her own humble position in society (Luke 1:48). Young and limited in every observable way Mary may have been. But God saw into her depths and knew that she was the person to whom he could entrust the bearing and raising of his Son.

And she did a fantastic job.

Reflected in Her Son

How do we know? Why, just look at Jesus. Granted, some saintly persons have mediocre parents. But from Jesus' integrity, steadiness, compassion, and courage, the logical conclusion is that his mother—and foster father—raised him well. Granted also that Jesus was perfect necessarily: he was the Son of God. But while remaining fully God, he became fully human, and so he grew up in a normal way. Like any boy, he learned from what he experienced and was taught. He matured through obeying and facing hardship (see Luke 2:40, 52; Hebrews 5:8). As we meet him in the Gospels, then, Jesus reflects both his Father in heaven and his mother and foster father in Nazareth. It's easy to imagine the neighbors in town watching Jesus handle a situation and remarking to one another, "That's *just* the kind of thing Mary would have done," or "He reminded me of Joseph when he said that."

From the reflection of Mary in her son we can be confident that she fulfilled her assignment well, but we cannot get a distinct sense of her as a person. Happily, however, the evangelists recount some episodes in her life. Matthew and Luke include her in their Gospels because they were concerned with the question of Jesus' origins, and Mary is part of that answer. But Luke also shows an interest in Mary in her own right, as does John. Both Luke and John present a sketch of Mary as, in some sense, Jesus' ideal disciple, and both depict her as a lasting gift to us, his followers. This is not to say that they paint a detailed portrait of Mary. But the little they tell us invites us to pay attention to her.

Six Episodes in Mary's Life

In this book, we respond to the evangelists' invitation. Within the format of the Six Weeks with the Bible series, we have six sessions to work with. We will use them to explore the episodes in Mary's life in the Gospels of Luke and John. We will look at the one scene in which Mary appears in Mark's Gospel (Mark 3:21–35; page 78). Because of space limitations, we do not try to examine Mary in Matthew's Gospel, so we won't be reading about the visit of the Magi or the holy family's flight to Egypt. For those incidents, you might look at *Joy to the World*, the Six Weeks volume on Matthew 1–2 and Luke 1–2 by Louise Perrotta (full disclosure: my lovely wife). Also because of space limitations, we do not look at the foreshadowings of Mary in the Old Testament or at the radiant image of her in the book of Revelation (Revelation 12:1–17). We will, however, consider aspects of Mary's life that the Gospels do not deal with explicitly: her being conceived without the disorder of original sin, her remaining always a virgin, her being taken up into heaven at the end of her life, and her maternal role in the family of Jesus' followers.

The World She Lived In

To get a rounded view of Mary, it is helpful to know a little about the world she lived in. Let's start with geography. Mary's home town, Nazareth, was a farming village on a hillside in northern Palestine, in the region called Galilee. About ten miles away, on the next line of hills to the north, lay Cana, another farming village, where Mary and Jesus attended a wedding. In Mary's day, if you traveled from Nazareth and Cana to explore the rest of Galilee, you would mostly find similar villages. Galilee was a rural area, with only two or three small cities—a backwater kind of place.

We will observe Mary traveling to Jerusalem and Bethlehem. Both places were some eighty to ninety miles south of Nazareth. Jerusalem was the historical capital of the Jews and the site of the temple, the focal point of Jewish worship. Bethlehem, a smaller town, was just five miles south of Jerusalem. Probably just to the west of Jerusalem was the unnamed "Judean town" where Mary visited her relative Elizabeth.

In all likelihood, Mary traveled back and forth between these places on foot, because that is how most people got around in those days. Like any peasant woman of her time, Mary undoubtedly did a lot of walking in her life. If we try to picture her trips with Joseph to Bethlehem or Jerusalem, and even to Egypt and back, we should probably forget about the image of her riding on a donkey.

The Work She Did

From the hill where Nazareth is located, you can see the best farmland in Israel: the flat Jezreel Valley. In its rich soil people have raised abundant crops of barley and wheat for thousands of years. The residents of first-century Nazareth were too poor to own such desirable land. On their hillside, the soil is thin, and bedrock shows through here and there. They did not have an easy life, wresting a living from such ground.

The Nazarenes' survival strategy involved building terraces on their hillside. Stones, at least, were in abundant supply. The villagers broke them into pieces about the size and shape of an American football and constructed low walls, behind which they layered soil and gravel. The soil had to be carried up the hill in baskets borne by donkeys—or on people's heads. Shallow terraces were sufficient for grains and grapevines. Deeper terraces were needed for olive and fig trees. For vegetables and beans, which need more water, the villagers carved terraces right into the bedrock, creating large, flat planters. From higher up on the hillside they cut basins to catch rainwater and carved little irrigation channels leading down into the terraces, to coax the water to the roots of the plants. It was a labor-intensive approach to farming. But, besides rock, their own labor was the only major resource that the residents of Nazareth had at their disposal.

Joseph, Mary, and Jesus undoubtedly shared in this work. Joseph, and Jesus after him, was the village carpenter (Mark 6:3). But in a small village—Nazareth had, perhaps, four hundred residents—there wasn't enough business for full-time tradespeople. One man might have a part-time specialty in carpentry, another in leather working or making pots or raising doves; but everyone would be involved in the work of terracing and irrigation, sowing and reaping, and caring for livestock. Joseph would have farmed like everyone else. Mary would have spent hours out on the hillside with the other women of the village, watering lentils, pasturing goats, and shaking ripe olives from the trees onto the ground at harvest time. Among the terraces where they grew grapes, the villagers carved a wide, shallow depression into the bedrock for crushing grapes for wine. We might picture Jesus there, trampling grapes and singing harvest songs with the other teens of Nazareth.

Home and Family

The residents of Nazareth eked out a minimal existence. From what archaeologists have found, no one was wealthy. The villagers lived in small, one- or two-room stone houses with thatched roofs. Built directly on the surface of the bedrock, the houses had rough stone floors. Under the floors were cellars, which residents of centuries past had carved into the rock. The cellars were connected to each other by tunnels. In some cases, a second or even third level of cellars was carved out in the rock. In these underground chambers the Nazarenes kept their grains, beans, figs, and jars of oil and wine.

The houses had small courtyards where families worked, cooked, and ate. In one courtyard, excavators found small holes bored into the surface of the rock to hold the timbers of a press for squeezing olives for oil.

In Palestine in the first century, the basic social unit was the extended family—older couple, married sons and their wives and children, and other relatives. Members of each extended family tended to live close together. Artists might depict Mary, Joseph, and Jesus as living in some spacious, isolated setting, but almost certainly they lived in a small house, with members of their extended family nearby.

There was no village bakery in Nazareth. Each house would have had its own oven. Archaeologists have discovered one, an arched niche carved into the rocky hillside. Like the other women of the village, Mary would have used her oven each day to bake her family's daily bread.

Thus, if we wish to imagine the setting of Mary's life, we should picture a village of small houses crowded together, with people living in close quarters, sheep and goats wandering around—a busy, noisy, pungent, sociable place. There are many villages like that in the developing world today.

A Woman of Psalm 1

What can we know about Mary from the culture of the time? The likelihood that a poor girl in first-century Nazareth would know how to read is very low. Mary lived in a society in which few people knew how to read, and almost none of them women, let alone peasant girls. But this does not mean that she was uneducated. Scripture was read and explained on the Sabbath. Regular pilgrimages to the temple in Jerusalem were opportunities for learning. As we will see, Luke portrays Mary as having a considerable knowledge of Scripture, as well as a Spirit-guided sensitivity for responding to it. I like to think of Mary as a "woman of Psalm 1": she listened to the law of the Lord with joy; she remembered it and meditated on it day and night (see Psalm 1:2).

As mentioned already, Mary may not have been more than thirteen when the angel Gabriel appeared to her. It was normal for families to arrange the marriage of a daughter as she reached puberty. Betrothal constituted the marital commitment, but customarily the young woman would continue to live in her parents' home for another year before moving to her husband's home and consummating the marriage. It is during that year of betrothal that we meet Mary in Luke's Gospel.

Documents and Tradition

Besides the Gospels, do other sources tell us anything about Mary's life? Perhaps a little, but their reliability is difficult to assess. The earliest possible source of information, coming from the second century, is a short narrative called the *Protogospel of James*. It purports to tell about Mary's parents, childhood, and early life with Joseph. The document may contain traces of historical traditions. It depicts Jesus' being born in a cave, a detail that finds support in the writings of a second-century Palestinian Christian named Justin. It is the *Protogospel* that gives us the names of Mary's parents, Joachim and Anna. It is also the first witness to Mary's perpetual virginity. But the *Protogospel* is not a reliable source from which to construct a portrait of Mary. At key points it conflicts with the Gospels. Mary's parents, for example, are depicted as exceedingly wealthy, whereas Luke portrays Mary and Joseph as quite poor. The document emphasizes that Joseph and Mary are not married, yet Matthew and Luke make it clear that they were husband and wife. The *Protogospel* shows confusion about historical matters, such as Jewish customs, and contains seemingly imaginary elements. Although some details in the *Protogospel* have been taken up into Christian tradition, the early Church excluded it from the New Testament.

Even though we lack other early written sources for Mary's life, certain elements of the church's tradition not contained in the Gospels do expand and deepen our understanding of her. We will explore some of these in the course of this book.

A final note before we begin. Luke and John have given us miniature narratives of events in Mary's life. Compared with a modern news report or short story, the accounts are very sparse. The evangelists have gotten to the heart of events as simply and directly as possible. That is helpful for our understanding, yet it means that we lack many of the details that we might expect or want. Consequently, we have to put our imaginations to work. In the "Exploring the Theme" sections, I have done a little creative thinking about how events might have unfolded. But my ideas are merely suggestive. It is up to you, the reader, to picture the scenes for yourself in order to see Mary of Nazareth more clearly and deeply.

ANGELIC ANNOUNCEMENTS

Questions to Begin

10 minutes
Use a question or two to get warmed up for the reading.

1 What is your favorite picture or statue of Mary?

2 Have you ever felt the presence of an angel?

O God, who willed that your Word
should take on the reality of human flesh
in the womb of the Virgin Mary,
grant, we pray,
that we, who confess our Redeemer to be God and man,
may merit to become partakers even in his divine nature.

Collect prayer, Mass of the Annunciation

10 minutes
Read the passage aloud. Let individuals take turns
reading paragraphs.

The Background

Luke begins his Gospel by telling us of two angelic announcements. There are a number of similarities between the two scenes, and the similarities serve to highlight the differences. What similarities and differences do you notice? What significance do they have?

The Reading: Luke 1:5–38

An Old Woman Will Bear a Son!

1:5 In the days of King Herod of Judea, there was a priest named Zechariah, who belonged to the priestly order of Abijah. His wife was a descendant of Aaron, and her name was Elizabeth. 6 Both of them were righteous before God, living blamelessly according to all the commandments and regulations of the Lord. 7 But they had no children, because Elizabeth was barren, and both were getting on in years.

8 Once when he was serving as priest before God and his section was on duty, 9 he was chosen by lot, according to the custom of the priesthood, to enter the sanctuary of the Lord and offer incense. 10 Now at the time of the incense-offering, the whole assembly of the people was praying outside. 11 Then there appeared to him an angel of the Lord, standing at the right side of the altar of incense. 12 When Zechariah saw him, he was terrified; and fear overwhelmed him. 13 But the angel said to him, "Do not be afraid, Zechariah, for your prayer has been heard. Your wife Elizabeth will bear you a son, and you will name him John. 14 You will have joy and gladness, and many will rejoice at his birth, 15 for he will be great in the sight of the Lord. He must never drink wine or strong drink; even before his birth he will be filled with the Holy Spirit. 16 He will turn many of the people of Israel to the Lord their God. 17 With the spirit and power of Elijah he will go before him, to turn the hearts of parents to their children, and the disobedient to the wisdom of the righteous, to make ready a people prepared for the Lord." 18 Zechariah said to the angel, "How will I know that this is so? For I am an old man, and my wife is getting on in years." 19 The angel replied, "I am Gabriel. I stand in the presence of God, and I have been sent to speak to you and to bring you this good news. 20 But now, because you did not believe my words, which will be fulfilled in their time, you will become mute, unable to speak, until the day these things occur."

²¹ Meanwhile the people were waiting for Zechariah, and wondered at his delay in the sanctuary. ²² When he did come out, he could not speak to them, and they realized that he had seen a vision in the sanctuary. He kept motioning to them and remained unable to speak. ²³ When his time of service was ended, he went to his home.

²⁴ After those days his wife Elizabeth conceived, and for five months she remained in seclusion. She said, ²⁵ "This is what the Lord has done for me when he looked favorably on me and took away the disgrace I have endured among my people."

A Virgin Will Bear a Son!

²⁶ In the sixth month the angel Gabriel was sent by God to a town in Galilee called Nazareth, ²⁷ to a virgin engaged to a man whose name was Joseph, of the house of David. The virgin's name was Mary. ²⁸ And he came to her and said, "Greetings, favored one! The Lord is with you." ²⁹ But she was much perplexed by his words and pondered what sort of greeting this might be. ³⁰ The angel said to her, "Do not be afraid, Mary, for you have found favor with God. ³¹ And now, you will conceive in your womb and bear a son, and you will name him Jesus. ³² He will be great, and will be called the Son of the Most High, and the Lord God will give to him the throne of his ancestor David. ³³ He will reign over the house of Jacob forever, and of his kingdom there will be no end." ³⁴ Mary said to the angel, "How can this be, since I am a virgin?" ³⁵ The angel said to her, "The Holy Spirit will come upon you, and the power of the Most High will overshadow you; therefore the child to be born will be holy; he will be called Son of God. ³⁶ And now, your relative Elizabeth in her old age has also conceived a son; and this is the sixth month for her who was said to be barren. ³⁷ For nothing will be impossible with God." ³⁸ Then Mary said, "Here am I, the servant of the Lord; let it be with me according to your word." Then the angel departed from her.

First Impression

5 minutes
Briefly mention a question you have about the reading or one thing in it that surprised, impressed, delighted, or challenged you. No discussion! Just listen to one another's reactions.

If participants have not read this section already, read it aloud.
Otherwise go on to "Questions for Reflection and Discussion."

A Surprise for Zechariah

Luke 1:5–25. It is time for the afternoon sacrifice. A flickering fire crowns the high, open-air altar in front of the temple. The crowd begins to chant prayers. An old man, the priest Zechariah, climbs the steps to the temple's entrance, passes through the ornate curtain across the doorway, and is lost from sight.

Inside the dimly lit chamber, Zechariah drops a few grains of incense on the burning coals of another, smaller altar. A cloud of smoke bursts upward—and an angel appears!

Luke does not describe the angel, but the angel's awesomeness is reflected in the priest's reaction: he is terrified. The angel, however, has not come to proclaim woe but to deliver good news. Zechariah's elderly wife is going to have a baby. *Elizabeth? But that's impossible*, the old priest thinks, and as he listens to the angel's description of the child's future, his fear ebbs and skepticism flows in. When the angel is finished speaking, Zechariah asks, in effect, "How can I know what you're telling me is true?"

One imagines a sudden widening of the angel's eyes. "I bring a message from *God*," he declares, "and *you* will be struck speechless until it is fulfilled." If the old priest wanted a sign to confirm the angel's message, there it is. He stumbles out to the steps and gesticulates to the waiting crowd, trying to convey the encounter he has just experienced.

This is surprising. What follows is more surprising still.

The Story Shifts

Luke 1:26–38. Suppose you're watching a documentary about some crucial moment in American history. In the opening scenes, you see government officials gravely conferring at the White House. Suddenly the scene shifts to a mobile home in a small Arkansas town, and you watch a teenage girl humming a tune while she bathes her dog. *What is this?* you wonder. *Has somebody's YouTube video gotten mixed into the documentary? What does this girl have to do with a national crisis?*

A first-time reader turning the page from Zechariah's encounter with the angel might feel a similar puzzlement. The imposing temple and the senior priest disappear. The scene shifts from the historic city of Jerusalem to a remote hillside village. Inside a small, thatched-roof house, a very young woman comes into view. *Is this the same story?* the reader might wonder.

In fact, Zechariah's meeting with the angel was just the lead-in. The real story begins here.

Gabriel's Visit

As Luke introduces this young woman, he underlines her low place in society by saying nothing about her family—in effect, he omits her surname—and identifying her simply as Mary. Yet God has sent Gabriel to her, too, and the angel addresses her with greater respect than he showed Zechariah: "Favored one!"

Mary is taken aback—not by the angel but by the greeting. "Favored one!" Who was ever addressed by God or angel like that? Why, no one in Scripture! Some Old Testament figures were said to enjoy God's favor, for example, Noah and Moses; but they were called to pivotal roles in God's plans (Genesis 6:8; Exodus 33:12). And what about the rest of the angel's greeting: "The Lord is with you"? That was something said to a soldier going into battle. It meant, "Be brave! God will help you!" Saul said it to David before he went out to meet Goliath (see 1 Samuel 17:37). What could the angel's greeting mean except that Mary is about to receive a great and difficult mission? Mary knows her Bible, and her mind works quickly. In a flash she is puzzled and frightened.

"Stop being afraid," the angel tells Mary (that's the nuance in the Greek). "You will bear a son who will be the salvation of his people."

What Mary does not say in response to this amazing announcement is quite revealing. She does not ask the angel what he means, probably because, as a devout Jew, she is familiar with the divine promises that the angel has indicated will now be fulfilled. Nor does she try to get out of the responsibility—unlike Moses at the burning bush, who made numerous objections to God's call and finally begged God to pick someone else (Exodus 3:10–4:13). Mary does not even express astonishment that God has chosen *her*. There is no "Who am I?" or "You've got to be kidding!"—perhaps because a knowledge of God's graciousness to her is already the bedrock of her life. Above all, unlike someone else we just read about, she doesn't ask, "How can I know what you're telling me is true?"

A Question and an Answer

Mary does have a question, though. God's call, as the angel has delivered it, seems to be urgent: "You *will* conceive . . . you *will* bear. . . you *will* name . . ." The announcement sounds like a call to immediate action. Mary is well aware that God does not issue postdated commands. Did he tell Noah, "In a year or so I want you to start building an ark"? Mary feels impelled to carry out the divine command at once—but how? She is only engaged, and the wedding is at some time in the future. She is ready to do what God wants. But what can that be?

The angel explains that she will become pregnant through the power of God's Spirit. This answers Mary's question with an astonishing mystery to ponder: her son will not only be the expected savior of his people; he will be God's Son in a unique way. But now is the moment not for pondering but for deciding. Mary has been told what God is going to do, yet God is not forcing her to cooperate. She is free to decline. Only if she assents will her mission begin to unfold. The angel is waiting for an answer.

"Let it be with me according to your word."

Mary's response echoes what the angel has just said to her, for his affirmation that "nothing will be impossible with God" is, more literally, "no *word* from God will be powerless." The echo expresses the perfect fit between God's call and Mary's response. She is totally willing to play her part in God's plan. Her answer also expresses her belief that God's word *is* all powerful, that God accomplishes whatever he sets out to do. Thus, her simple "Let it be with me according to your word" expresses both her obedience and her faith.

Reflections on the Reading

Mary's ready response to God's call could come only from a heart already wide open to God. Yet we should not confuse total surrender with complete comprehension. She is very young, and there is much that she does not yet understand about the divine plan into which she has been drawn. The angel has described the mission of her son in scriptural terms. To a pious Jew his words might indicate that God is about to initiate the national liberation that many hoped for on the basis of their understanding of Scripture. In time, Jesus will correct that misinterpretation, for he has come to accomplish something greater than that. His disciples will have to go through the process of learning the deeper meaning of God's promises to Israel. Probably Mary, too, will have to undergo this process of relinquishment to grasp both the suffering and the glory of God's plans through her son.

At the moment, however, Mary is filled with wonder at what has just taken place, as she will tell Elizabeth, in our reading for next week. Speaking of Elizabeth, notice the angel's final words, which connect his announcement to Mary with his announcement to Zechariah. Eventually, the son to be born to Elizabeth and Zechariah—John the Baptist—will prepare the way for Mary's son: John will "make ready a people prepared for the Lord."

Luke has described two angelic announcements, and he invites us to compare the recipients. One is an honored priest in the capital city; the other, a seemingly insignificant young woman in a rural village. God is surprisingly kind to the priest, but he is staggeringly favorable to the young woman. Luke is showing us something about God here that deserves careful pondering.

Also worth pondering are the human responses. The same angel, Gabriel, appears to both Zechariah and Mary, but they respond differently. Zechariah can't get over the seeming impossibility of a child being born to his elderly wife. Mary simply accepts the angel's declaration that nothing is impossible to God. In their spontaneous reactions to Gabriel's unexpected appearance, we get a glimpse of the relationship of each person with God. Zechariah's response is what we might expect of an ordinarily good person who nevertheless lacks a certain intimacy with God. Mary's trusting and obedient response comes from a heart turned toward God, a heart that embraces God's immense goodness and trustworthiness without reservation.

45 minutes
Choose questions according to your interest and time.

1 Some differences between the angel's announcement to Zechariah and to Mary are mentioned in "Exploring the Theme." Can you find others? What do they indicate about the two sons to be born? What do they indicate about Mary and her relationship with God?

2 God might have sent Gabriel to Zechariah at any time. Why do you think he sent him when Zechariah was working in the temple?

3 Zechariah's being struck speechless is a sign for him but also a punishment. Does it seem like an appropriate punishment?

4 Do you ever feel that you are too far from what's happening in the world for God to take much interest in what you do with your life? How might this view affect how you live? What does this reading say about that view?

5 Gabriel visits Zechariah in a place and at a time of prayer. Although we might picture Mary as praying at the moment the angel appears to her, we might equally picture her—as in some artistic representations—as sewing or, as the local tradition in Nazareth goes, drawing water from the town's spring. Luke depicts her simply as being in Nazareth, a village where people are going about their ordinary lives. Compare Jesus' call to Peter and companions while they are at work (Luke 5:1–11). When have you become aware of God's presence in the midst of your ordinary activities? What can help a person be attentive to God as he or she goes through the day?

6 At the time, most people would probably have regarded the priest Zechariah as more likely than the young woman Mary to have something to say about God and his ways. Would they have been correct? What factors may cause us to ignore a person's spiritual depth and wisdom?

7 Notice the angel's references to the action of the Holy Spirit (verses 15 and 35). How have you experienced the Holy Spirit? What difference does the Holy Spirit make in a person's life? How can a person be open to the presence of the Spirit?

8 Mary's unrehearsed response to the angel's surprise announcement lets us see something of the kind of person she is. When have you witnessed an unexpected event that suddenly brings a person's character to light? When have you experienced this in yourself? What did you learn from this?

9 **Focus question.** What point in this week's reading strikes you most personally? How might this be God's word to you? How could you respond to it?

Prayer to Close

10 minutes
Use this approach—or create your own!

◆ The Angelus, a prayer traditionally prayed each day at noon:

Leader: The Angel of the Lord declared unto Mary.

Response: And she conceived of the Holy Spirit.

Hail Mary, full of grace . . .

Leader: Behold the handmaid of the Lord.

Response: Be it done unto me according to thy word.

Hail Mary . . .

Leader: And the Word was made Flesh.

Response: And dwelt among us.

Hail Mary . . .

Leader: Pray for us, O Holy Mother of God.

Response: That we may be made worthy of the promises of Christ.

Living Tradition

Full of Grace

S aints point to Jesus, not to themselves. If visitors to Mother Teresa's center for the destitute dying in Calcutta began to sing her praises, she would cut them off with a remark such as, "It's Jesus' work we're doing." When people came to Brother André Bessette seeking prayers for healing, he would tell them to ask St. Joseph to pray for them. That way they would associate any healing with St. Joseph's intercession. If someone nevertheless suggested that Brother André's prayers had special power, he would become irritated and scold them.

I can't picture Mary snapping at anyone. But I'm sure she never tried to draw attention to herself. When Elizabeth congratulated her for being chosen to bear the Savior, Mary answered, in effect, "The Lord has indeed been good to me. Praise *him!*" We may suppose that was how she responded to others who later fussed over her because of her son. Or perhaps her response was along the lines of "Blessed? Yes, I'm richly blessed. And so is everyone who believes God's word and obeys him" (see Luke 11:27–28).

Mary would have wanted people to think about God and Jesus, because that was where her thoughts were directed. That is what we see at the Annunciation, when she tells Gabriel that she is wide open to whatever God has in mind for her. In the scenes from her life in John's Gospel, one can sense her communion of thought and feeling with her son. The result of Mary's focus on Jesus is that she has a kind of transparency to him: the more closely you look at her, the more clearly you see Jesus—and the Father who called her and the Spirit who filled her.

Mary's transparency to the Lord is especially apparent at the beginning and end of her life—her being conceived without original sin and being taken up bodily into heaven. These aspects of her life are sometimes called "the glories of Mary." But because they were not her doing but God's gifts to her, they are a kind of window into God's glory. The more we ponder these aspects of her life, the more we are led to an awareness of God's love—for Mary, but also for us.

Mary's Immaculate Conception

The first of these gifts to Mary is called her "immaculate conception" (for the second, her assumption into heaven, see p. 90). To understand what it meant for her—and what it means for us—we need to step back and consider events that took place all the way at the beginning of human existence.

The opening chapters of the Bible tell us that God made humanity very good but that the first humans broke their relationship with him. The story in Genesis 3 symbolizes people's refusal to trust that God had their best interests at heart. They overstepped the limits of their creaturely status and put themselves in the position of making their own moral norms—of deciding what was good and bad for them despite God's word. This rebellion against God triggered a tsunami within them that shattered their inner peace and devastated their relationships with one another. Their inner harmony of mind and heart, of inner drives and will, disintegrated. Their natural tendencies, now badly directed and ill controlled, began to lead them astray from the life God had created them for.

The first humans' "fallen" condition has been passed on to us, their descendants. Theologians call it "original sin." The term is a shorthand way of saying "the present internally divided condition of humanity due to the sin committed by the first humans." You can read about it in Paul's letter to the Romans (Romans 5:12–21) and in the *Catechism of the Catholic Church* (sections 390–409). As the *Catechism* explains, original sin is a sin only by analogy; it is not a sinful act we commit but a condition that we inherit (section 404).

The Sin Problem

Original sin, along with its consequences—our particular sins against one another, our vulnerability to being deceived by the devil, the inevitability of death—is exactly what God sent his Son to save us from. The Son took on our human nature so that, as a human being, he might reverse our ancestors' rebellion and free us from its consequences. In place of pride and violation of God's word, Jesus demonstrated humility and obedience to God. Rather than distrusting God, he trusted God even to the point of giving up his life on a cross in submission to the Father's plan. Now that he has died and risen as one of us, he is the road by which each of us can walk in repentance and enter a new relationship with God—Jesus' own relationship with God. In this new life, our inner disorder is set right, and God's Spirit empowers us to live the good life for which God has called us into existence. In other words, through Jesus original sin is removed. This does not mean that we are instantly perfected. But a fundamental change occurs within us. Set right with God and within ourselves, we begin the process of growth that will lead to our becoming finally, in God's eternal kingdom, everything he wants us to be.

Against this background, we can grasp the meaning of Mary's being immaculately conceived: God allowed her to experience, ahead of time, the full effects of her Son's removal of original sin. From the first instant of her existence, she was preserved from the interior disorder that we experience because of original sin. St. Paul declared that God "has blessed us in Christ with every spiritual blessing . . . as he chose us in Christ before the foundation of the world to be holy and blameless before him in love" (Ephesians 1:3–4). Mary experienced this being chosen beforehand, this being made holy and blameless, in a unique way.

Because Mary did not suffer from original sin, she was entirely free to choose to obey or disobey God. And, in fact, with God's help, she did always obey him, from the heart. "By the grace of God Mary remained free of every personal sin her whole life long," the *Catechism* states, summing up the Catholic tradition (section 493). God's purpose was that Mary would be perfectly suited for her assignment: bearing and raising his Son as a human being.

God Chose Us, Too

God's goodness to Mary demonstrates his goodness to all of us. Mary experienced in a unique way the grace of God that is his gift to all. Her immaculate conception stands as the supreme illustration of the fact that God chose *each one of us* before bringing us into existence, with the intention that each one of us would live in a communion of trust and obedience with him. To attain this purpose, God gave his Son as an atoning sacrifice to remove the condition of original sin from each one of us, so that we might become "holy and blameless before him in love."

St. Paul encourages us to "work out your own salvation with fear and trembling; for it is God who is at work in you, enabling you both to will and to work for his good pleasure" (Philippians 2:12–13). To *always* want and will what God wanted and willed was the grace that God gave Mary from her first moment. That gift to her is a sign of the grace God gives to us every day. Mary's immaculate conception is testimony to God's graciousness, a reminder that we have a life with God not because we love God but because God loved us first (see 1 John 4:10).

Where Did This Doctrine Come From?

Not all of this is explicitly stated in the New Testament. So it is fair to ask how the belief in Mary's immaculate conception originated and what connection it has with the Gospels. Basically, what happened is that, guided by the Spirit, Christians reflected on Mary as she is portrayed in the Gospels. Her perfect cooperation with God—"Let it be with me according to your word"—made a profound impression on those who pondered it. As Christians reflected on her story, certain details seemed to have a great depth of meaning— above all, Gabriel's greeting, "Favored one!" Literally, the Greek word means "having been favored." No one else is addressed this way in Scripture; thus, the greeting implies that Mary is the object of God's favor to an extraordinary degree. Her being most favored by God could only mean that she was the greatest recipient of God's gifts, the clearest mirror of his goodness. The person on whom God's favor rested perfectly was his own Son (Luke 3:22). If Mary, too, was highly favored, she must somehow share in Jesus' perfect harmony with the Father.

Converging with these ponderings were reflections from another direction: it would be fitting for the Son of God to take flesh from a woman who was free of humanity's fallen condition. It would be appropriate for the person who would have the most direct impact on the Son of God's formation as a child to be totally in tune with God's will at every level of her being.

Thus, in the minds of the early Christians, the idea that Mary was preserved from original sin from the first moment of her existence seemed to be implied by the portrait of her in the gospels, by Gabriel's greeting to her, and by the requirements of her mission. In fact, Christians from East to West arrived at the conviction that she was immaculately conceived. In the fourth century St. Ephrem of Syria testified to Mary's immaculate conception in a hymn declaring that Mary was free of any flaw or stain. In eighth-century Palestine, St. John of Damascus celebrated it in a homily on the nativity. Franciscan theologians in the thirteenth century worked out a way to state that the merits of Christ's death were granted to Mary ahead of time to prepare her for her role as his mother. In the Western Church, an annual feast of Mary's immaculate conception was placed on the calendar in the fifteenth century. In the nineteenth century, Pope Pius IX affirmed that this centuries-long tradition is, indeed, an integral element of Christian faith.

Mary, Give us a heart as beautiful, pure, and spotless as yours. A heart like yours, so full of love and humility. May we be able to receive Jesus as the Bread of Life, to love Him as you loved Him, to serve Him under the mistreated face of the poor. We ask this through Jesus Christ our Lord. Amen

Mother Teresa of Calcutta

A VISIT IN HASTE

Questions to Begin

10 minutes
Use a question or two to get warmed up for the reading.

1 When was the last time you had an unexpected guest—or were an unexpected guest?

2 Has a piece of good news recently brought you joy?

She went "with haste" to visit her cousin Elizabeth. As she made her way . . . southward to Judea and traversed the Holy Land, where almost every inch of ground evoked a sacred memory, scriptural passages came crowding in her mind. . . . Enlightened by the invisible presence of the Messias in her womb, the whole array of Old Testament promises took on for her a new and deeper meaning. The ground itself under her feet seemed to be vibrant with life, so full of joy and expectation was she.

M. M. Philipon, *The Mother of God*

10 minutes
Read the passage aloud. Let individuals take turns
reading paragraphs.

The Reading: Luke 1:39–56

Kinswomen—and Unborn Babies—Meet

1:39 In those days Mary set out and went with haste to a Judean town in the hill country, 40 where she entered the house of Zechariah and greeted Elizabeth. 41 When Elizabeth heard Mary's greeting, the child leaped in her womb. And Elizabeth was filled with the Holy Spirit 42 and exclaimed with a loud cry, "Blessed are you among women, and blessed is the fruit of your womb. 43 And why has this happened to me, that the mother of my Lord comes to me? 44 For as soon as I heard the sound of your greeting, the child in my womb leaped for joy. 45 And blessed is she who believed that there would be a fulfillment of what was spoken to her by the Lord."

Acknowledging God's Goodness

46 And Mary said, "My soul magnifies the Lord,
47 and my spirit rejoices in God my Savior,
48 for he has looked with favor on the lowliness of his servant.
   Surely, from now on all generations will call me blessed;
49 for the Mighty One has done great things for me,
   and holy is his name.
50 His mercy is for those who fear him
   from generation to generation.
51 He has shown strength with his arm;
   he has scattered the proud in the thoughts of their hearts.
52 He has brought down the powerful from their thrones,
   and lifted up the lowly;
53 he has filled the hungry with good things,
   and sent the rich away empty.
54 He has helped his servant Israel,
   in remembrance of his mercy,
55 according to the promise he made to our ancestors,
   to Abraham and to his descendants forever."

An Extended Stay

⁵⁶ And Mary remained with her about three months and then returned to her home.

First Impression

5 minutes
Briefly mention a question you have about the reading or one thing in it that surprised, impressed, delighted, or challenged you. No discussion! Just listen to one another's reactions.

If participants have not read this section already, read it aloud.
Otherwise go on to "Questions for Reflection and Discussion."

A Visit to Elizabeth

At the end of his announcement to Mary, Gabriel added a piece
of news of lesser importance but amazing in its own way. Mary's
"relative" Elizabeth is pregnant. Luke uses a general Greek word
for "kinswoman," not the word meaning "cousin." Much older than
Mary, Elizabeth is more like her aunt, or even her great-aunt. "Aunt
Betty's going to have a baby! I must go and see her." Mary will need
a companion, because a teenage girl can hardly travel the roads of
Palestine alone. Nevertheless, she quickly persuades her family to
make the arrangements and let her go.

     Mary sets out in haste, but she has a good four days of
walking ahead of her—an opportunity to ponder the new life within
her and to think about Elizabeth. The older woman has become
like a new Sarah—the great matriarch of the Bible who was
unexpectedly blessed with motherhood. But how, in God's plan,
is Elizabeth's pregnancy related to Mary's? The angel implied that
Elizabeth is someone Mary can confide in. Perhaps when they put
their stories together, the larger picture will emerge.

"The Mother of My Lord Comes to Me"

Zechariah and Elizabeth's house has been unusually subdued ever
since the angel silenced the old priest. But as soon as Mary walks
in the door, the Spirit-inspired squirming of Elizabeth's unborn child
alerts her to the presence of the Lord in her niece, and she shatters
the quiet with whoops of astonishment. "Your destiny is more
exalted than that of any other woman! You are blessed for believing
what God told you!" Mary has not come looking for confirmation
of the angel's message, but she gets it anyway. She cannot be
unmoved by the older woman's vehement congratulations. We
may suppose, however, that she is most touched by her aunt's
recognition of the child she is carrying: "The mother of my Lord
comes to me." Elizabeth acknowledges the mystery that has taken
place: Mary has become pregnant with the Son of God.

     Indeed, Mary responds, I *am* blessed. "The Mighty One has
done great things for me." Deeply stirred, her voice rises from the
level of conversation into prayer. Her words take the form of poetry,

of song—and, I suspect, it sounded more like black gospel music than monastic chant.

The Magnificat

Mary celebrates God's goodness not only to herself but also to the entire Jewish people. Her circle of concerns extends outward to embrace all who are poor, hungry, and oppressed. And her thanksgiving is remarkable for this: she speaks of God's salvation as a past event. God has removed the exploiters from the seats of authority; he has satisfied the hungry with good things. We have to remind ourselves that, as Mary prays, the emperor Augustus still rules in Rome; Herod continues on as the Romans' client king in Palestine. Peasants, laborers, and homeless people are no less miserable than they were a few days ago, before Gabriel appeared to her. "Mary," we might ask, "how can you thank God for already setting the world right, for bringing the fullness of his kingdom *now*?" Her answer would be simple: "My son, who is God's Son, will surely accomplish God's purposes. And he's here!"

An illiterate young woman from a small village would not be expected to utter a lengthy and quotable prayer. Yet Mary proclaims God's goodness with great beauty. Her prayer is full of echoes of the Bible, which tells us something about her. As her son was to observe, from the fullness of the heart the mouth speaks (Matthew 12:34).

Mary's vision of the work that God has under way goes beyond what Gabriel told her. Obviously, she has been thinking about the angel's message and has arrived at some insights. "Having heard that her child would be the son of David and Son of God, she translates this into good news for the lowly and the hungry and woe for the powerful and the rich," writes the New Testament scholar Raymond E. Brown. Yet her prayer may also suggest how much she does not yet understand. As another scholar, G. B. Caird, notes, if Mary's prayer "had been preserved as a separate psalm outside of its present context, we might have taken it to be a manifesto of a political and economic revolution." Quite possibly

Mary envisions her son bringing a national, political restoration to the Jewish people in their land, according to the common hope of Jews of the time.

Sharing Faith

Mary stays on with Elizabeth for three months. Origen, an early Church Father, offered a cheerful thought: if an hour with Mary and Jesus was a blessing for Elizabeth and John, how much more they would profit from three months of their presence! Guided by the Spirit, the two women have time to put their individual experiences of God together and to consider how they were connected. As they ponder God's actions, the two women form an icon of the Christian community soon to come into existence: the Church is the gathering of those who put their faith in God's word and praise him and share with one another their experiences of his presence, with Jesus himself present though unseen.

Mary returns home before her pregnancy becomes apparent. As she walks to Nazareth, she faces the prospect of explaining—or not explaining—her pregnancy to her family and to Joseph.

Reflections on the Reading

Mary thanks God for straightening out a world twisted by false values, by the exploitation of the weak by the strong. God has already begun to carry out this saving plan by his choice of Mary: she is insignificant from society's point of view but great from God's point of view because of her faith and her willingness to cooperate with him. In selecting her, God has bypassed those who seem great and wise in the world. God's setting things right in the human sphere begins here, with the incarnation of his Son in Mary of Nazareth. His saving plan will enter its definitive stage in Jesus' ministry, death, and resurrection. Today, by the gift of the Spirit to the Church, God's plan continues to unfold in and through us— regardless of whether we occupy important positions in society.

Questions for Reflection and Discussion

45 minutes
Choose questions according to your interest and time.

1 What reasons might Mary have had for going to visit Elizabeth?

2 How does Elizabeth know so much about what has been happening with Mary?

3 Mary says of God, "holy is his name" (Luke 1:49). Later Jesus will teach a prayer that begins, "Father, hallowed be your name" (Luke 11:2). Does Mary's prayer shed light on what it means to hallow God's name?

4 To judge from the rest of Mary's prayer, what does she mean when she says that she "magnifies" the Lord?

5 Mary says that she rejoices in God. What does it mean to rejoice in God? What is the connection between declaring God's greatness ("magnifying" God) and experiencing joy?

6 Do you find joy in God? Can a person choose to rejoice in God? What is the relationship between joy and sorrow in Christian life? See Luke 6:20–26.

7 How much is Mary's prayer—called the Magnificat—a part of your prayers? How much does it help to shape the way you pray at other times?

8 What impression of Mary do you get from our readings so far? What kind of person does she seem to be?

9 What could you do to cooperate with God's work of lifting up the lowly and filling the hungry with good things?

10 **Focus question.** Undoubtedly during her visit, Mary and Elizabeth talked with each other about what God is doing in their lives. Do you ever talk with others about what God is doing in your life? Have you found this to be easy? Difficult? A source of encouragement and faith?

Prayer to Close

10 minutes
Use this approach—or create your own!

♦ Pray Psalm 34 together. Perhaps divide into two groups and pray the verses alternately. Then take a few minutes to pray spontaneously for those who are needy or suffering in any way. End with an Our Father and a Hail Mary.

Or pray the Magnificat as it is often prayed in the Byzantine tradition: Between every two lines, pray: "More honorable than the cherubim, and beyond compare more glorious than the seraphim, who a virgin gave birth to God the Word—you, truly the Mother of God, we magnify." At the end, pray for those who are in need and conclude with an Our Father.

After visiting Elizabeth, Mary returned to Nazareth. When we see her next, she is on the road again, this time to Bethlehem, with her husband. In the six months between the two episodes, Mary and Joseph have gotten married.

Mary's marriage to Joseph meant that Jesus would know the love and care of a human father. Joseph was not stepfather to Jesus, because Jesus was not the child of another man. Nor was there any need for adoption, because Jesus was born into Joseph's marriage to Mary. Although Joseph was not biologically Jesus' father, he was to be Jesus' father in every other human way.

A Husband for Mary

But what did marriage to Joseph mean for Mary? Its most immediate effect was to avert the humiliation of an out-of-wedlock pregnancy. And it is possible that Joseph shielded Mary's honor at some cost to his own. Everyone in the village would be able to figure out that she had conceived the child before the wedding. They would assume that if Joseph thought another man was involved, he would have broken off the engagement. When he went ahead with the wedding, people might have concluded that he had fathered the child. Given the marriage-type commitment of betrothal, this would not have been wrong, but it would have been contrary to custom. Mary would have appreciated Joseph's willingness to bear any embarrassment her pregnancy occasioned.

Without Joseph, Mary would have gone on living with her family. Her father, brothers, uncles, and cousins would have helped to raise her son. How much better for her to have Joseph to depend on in the momentous task of—as someone has put it—teaching God how to be a human being.

Mary soon had to rely on Joseph in danger. Shortly after Jesus' birth, Herod plotted to kill him. Warned by an angel, Joseph demonstrated his reliability by quickly getting Mary and the child to safety. Thus, Mary trusted God to care for her, and God did care for her, through her husband. Reflecting on the holy family's flight to Egypt, Pope Leo XIII wrote, "In the miseries of the journey and the bitternesses of exile he was ever the companion, the assistance, and the upholder of the Virgin and of Jesus."

A Bond of Mutual Affection

One thing that marriage to Joseph did not mean for Mary was sexual relations. She remained a virgin (see page 56). Nonetheless, they had a real marriage. St. Thomas Aquinas pointed out that marriage "consists in an inseparable union of souls by which husband and wife are pledged to each other with a bond of mutual affection that cannot be sundered." Mary and Joseph certainly had that kind of relationship, Thomas insisted. Furthermore, he observed, the central labor of marriage is begetting and raising children, and, although Joseph and Mary did not beget any children, they raised Jesus—the most important piece of child rearing any married couple ever carried out.

Neither Leo nor Thomas viewed Joseph and Mary's marriage as a mere social convenience or practical help. Thomas discerned an "inseparable union of souls" and "bond of mutual affection" between them. Joseph was not only guardian and provider, in Leo's view; he was Mary's companion on the journey—not only the journey to Egypt but also the journey through life.

At first, Joseph was an outsider to the mystery of the incarnation that God had begun to unfold in his betrothed (Matthew 1:18–19). But then God brought Joseph in on the secret (Matthew 1:20–24). This put him in a position to be Mary's closest friend as she strove to respond to the unique vocation of motherhood to which God had called her. And she could be Joseph's friend, as he strove to respond to God's unique call to him.

In the Gospels we catch glimpses of the cooperation that developed between them. Their unusual way of observing the Old Testament law concerning the firstborn son (see Week 3) suggests that they examined Scripture together and reached an agreement about how to follow the law in regard to their very special firstborn.

When Jesus failed to join Mary and Joseph on the trip back home from the Passover in Jerusalem, they searched for him with shared anxiety, as any couple would: "Your father and I have been looking for you." Mary's words to Jesus in Jerusalem that day perhaps give us an insight into the couple's relationship with Jesus over the course of many years. As he did and said things that they did not expect, or, as in the temple incident, as he failed to do what they expected, Joseph and Mary must have searched together to understand him, trying to perceive how God wanted them to raise him and how God's plan was unfolding through him.

An Intimate Union

Pope Leo noted that "marriage is the most intimate of all unions" and "from its essence imparts a community of gifts between those that are joined together by it." Joseph, then, as Mary's husband, was "not only her life's companion, the witness of her maidenhood, the protector of her honor, but also, by virtue of the conjugal tie, a participator in her sublime dignity." Her dignity as mother of God, Leo noted, "is so lofty that nothing created can rank above it." Because Joseph was united to Mary by marriage, "it may not be doubted," Leo concluded, "that he approached nearer than any to the eminent dignity by which the Mother of God so nobly surpasses all created natures."

What this sharing of God's grace meant for Mary and Joseph we cannot know. Did they have a talky relationship? Or was much encompassed in an understanding silence? Who can say? In any case, Joseph must have been a joy for her. Elizabeth's recognition of God's favor toward her evoked the joyful Magnificat from Mary. What prayers of thanks must have bubbled up in her heart as she lived year after year with Joseph, the man who shared with her in the mystery of God's choosing her to bear and raise his Son!

The other side of the coin of marital love is the pain of bereavement. Joseph does not appear in the Gospels after the incident in which Jesus stayed behind in the temple. The common inference is that Joseph died before Jesus began his public mission. Mary, then, experienced the grief of widowhood.

Saint in the Making

Did Mary Change Her Thinking?

I n Mary's day, everyone in Nazareth, along with just about all the residents of Galilee and of Jerusalem and its surrounding area, were Jews. But Jews did not rule Palestine. Like every other land around the Mediterranean at that time, Palestine was ruled by Rome. This was a bitter pill for most Jews to swallow. Things would have been hard enough without the Romans. In the ancient world, most people were poor and life was a grind—and no existing technological, economic, or political means could change that. But Roman domination made things worse—and it had the sting of disappointment and shame. Jews treasured Scriptures in which, it seemed, God promised that they would live in their land in peace and unity under their own king. When Mary was growing up, some of the older adults in her life could remember when independent Jewish kings—the Maccabees—had in fact ruled in Jerusalem.

In Week 3, we will meet two pious Jews, Simeon and Anna, who are hoping for God to free his people and establish justice in their land. Simeon is looking forward to "the consolation of Israel," Anna to "the redemption of Jerusalem" (Luke 2:25, 38). These phrases commonly referred to the hoped-for liberation of and restoration of the Jewish people to their land.

Revolution in the Air

With the push of Roman oppression and the pull of aspirations for national restoration, Jews repeatedly took up arms against the Romans, believing that the moment of God's intervention had come. A couple of years after Jesus' birth, and again when he was about twelve years old, Jews in Galilee revolted—unsuccessfully.

In the Gospels we can see that hopes for national restoration were in the air during Jesus' public life. Crowds welcomed Jesus as a heaven-sent king, probably thinking that he had come to liberate them from the Romans (Matthew 21:9–10; John 6:15). His disciples looked forward to his establishing of a Jewish kingdom: they pictured him as king, with themselves as government ministers (Acts 1:6; Mark 10:35–37). Steering his listeners away from such a nationalistic understanding of his kingship was one of Jesus' most difficult and dangerous challenges. When people in his hometown realized that he had not come to restore the kingdom to Israel but rather to bring salvation to all peoples, they tried to kill him (Luke 4:23–30).

All this leads to the question: What did Mary think? Did she also look forward to God restoring freedom to the Jews in their ancestral land? We cannot know for sure. But it is reasonable to assume that she did share this expectation.

Political Expectations

In support of this assumption are Mary's name and the names of her family members. All were drawn from figures who had played a notable part in early Jewish history. Mary's name is a form of Miriam—the name of Moses' sister. Joseph was named after one of the sons of the patriarch Jacob. Other men in the family were also named after Israelite patriarchs: James (a form of Jacob), Joses (a form of Joseph), Simeon, and Judas (a form of Judah—Mark 6:3). Even Jesus fits this pattern. His name is a variant of Joshua—the man who had led the Israelite conquest of the land. Why are these names significant? During most of the Old Testament period, Jewish parents did not name their children after those great figures in Israel's early history. Jews adopted the practice, however, at the time of the Maccabees' movement for national restoration. The New Testament historian John Meier draws the following conclusion: "Most likely, therefore, the fact that all of Jesus' immediate family bear 'patriarchal' and 'matriarchal' names betokens the family's participation in this reawakening of Jewish national and religious identity." Because she came from a family that anticipated a God-given national restoration, it seems likely that Mary shared these expectations.

Such expectations would have shaped Mary's initial understanding of Gabriel's announcement to her. The angel's pronouncement that her son would sit on David's throne might sound like a declaration that he was going to fulfill the Jewish people's national aspirations.

Nothing in the Magnificat, the great prayer that Mary prays when she visits Elizabeth, stands against this assumption about Mary's thinking. In her prayer she celebrates what God has begun to do in the conception of her son—unseating tyrants and putting lowly but righteous people in control of society, distributing food to the poor, and letting excessive consumers go hungry. Mary rejoices that God is fulfilling "the promise he made to our ancestors, to Abraham and to his descendants forever" (Luke 1:55). God's promise to Abraham was that his descendants would possess the land. We can read the Magnificat as Mary's declaration that, through her divinely conceived son, God will fulfill this promise by breaking the Romans' grip on the land and putting the Jewish people in control again.

A Different Kind of Kingdom

The evangelists show Jesus instructing his disciples to relinquish a nationalistic understanding of God's plan of salvation. God was not going to bring his kingdom solely to the Jewish people, Jesus indicated; he was going to bring his kingdom to the whole world. As Messiah, Jesus was going to establish his reign not through military conquest but through death and resurrection. Although God's kingdom will ultimately overturn all injustice and sin (see Mark 13:26–27), in the meantime God will pour out his Holy Spirit to renew individuals and to create a new society in Christ (see Acts 1–2). How hard it was for Jesus' disciples to grasp this divine plan! Even after his resurrection people were asking him whether the moment for restoring the kingdom to Israel had arrived (Acts 1:6).

If Mary started out with the same expectations, she, too, must have gone through a process of relinquishing them. Somewhere between her joyous welcome of God's triumphant intervention on behalf of Israel in the Magnificat and her standing at her son's cross at Golgotha, Mary must have let go all expectations that Jesus was going to establish justice on earth by sweeping away Roman tyranny and restoring the kingdom to Israel.

There is no reason to think that Mary found this relinquishment of expectations easy. Her Magnificat shows a deep compassion and sense of solidarity with the poor and the oppressed. It seems clear that she longed intensely for God to establish justice in the world. She must have been pained to realize that the hungry and the oppressed were not soon to have the justice she longed for. I see no reason to think she would not have felt the pain of disappointment even as she began to grasp the plan that God was unfolding through his Son. In Gethsemane, Jesus himself felt almost crushed by sorrow at the prospect of his own suffering—and, we may suppose, at the prospect of the suffering of others that would be entailed in the coming of God's kingdom in the course of history. We may suppose that Mary had her own Gethsemane experience, it dawned on her that God intended to work through the cross—and that the time of the final coming of God's kingdom was a mystery not revealed to humans (Mark 13:32). For Mary, as for her son, the wisdom of the cross may have been almost too much to bear.

Surprised by God's Plan

The idea that Mary needed to change her thinking may be a little jarring. But Luke does not portray Mary as knowing everything from the outset. Quite the contrary, he repeatedly shows her surprised at the unfolding of God's plans. Twice he tells us that events spurred her to deep thought, undoubtedly because developments were not matching her expectations. On one of these occasions—the finding of Jesus in the temple—Jesus' words to his mother pretty clearly indicate that he thinks she needs to let go of her expectations regarding him (Luke 2:49). Mary is not diminished by the possibility of having to change her thinking. Compare John the Baptist. Jesus ranked John as the greatest prophet who ever lived—and he praised him precisely at the moment when John was wrestling with the fact that Jesus was not fulfilling his expectations (Luke 7:18–28).

The possibility that Mary had to let go of expectations for how God would act, and that she found this process difficult, only deepens the portrait of her humanity. In this way, it also makes her a more accessible model for us. We ourselves experience the need to change our thinking about God. Who has not at one time or another expected God to work in some way in our own life or in the life of someone near to us, only to discover that God did not intend to act that way? If Mary had to negotiate the process we face as disciples—needing to grow in our understanding of God, as well as his ways and his plans, and finding it hard to embrace the way of the cross—that makes her a sign of hope for us. It also makes her a sympathetic intercessor for us, when we find ourselves in this process.

GIVING BIRTH TO THE SAVIOR

Questions to Begin

10 minutes
Use a question or two to get warmed up for the reading.

1 On a trip, have you ever had to deal with accommodations that were far less than ideal?

2 Amid busyness and commercialism, what helps you keep Christ in Christmas?

**O God, who through the fruitful virginity of Blessed Mary
bestowed on the human race
the grace of eternal salvation,
grant, we pray,
that we may experience the intercession of her,
through whom we were found worthy
to receive the author of life.**

Collect prayer, Mass of Mary, Mother of God

10 minutes
Read the passage aloud. Let individuals take turns
reading paragraphs.

The Background

Elizabeth's baby has been born, and Zechariah has been released
from silence and has prayed a lengthy prayer—except for Jesus'
chapter-long prayer at the Last Supper in John's Gospel (John 17),
Zechariah's is the longest prayer in the New Testament. But he had
had plenty of time to think about what he was going say when he got
his voice back. In the prayer he foresees not only what God will call
his son to do but also what Mary's son, yet unborn, will do. It is the
arrival of Mary's son to which we now turn our attention.

The Reading: Luke 2:1–20

Mary Gives Birth

2:1 In those days a decree went out from Emperor Augustus that all
the world should be registered. 2 This was the first registration and
was taken while Quirinius was governor of Syria. 3 All went to their
own towns to be registered. 4 Joseph also went from the town of
Nazareth in Galilee to Judea, to the city of David called Bethlehem,
because he was descended from the house and family of David. 5 He
went to be registered with Mary, to whom he was engaged and who
was expecting a child. 6 While they were there, the time came for
her to deliver her child. 7 And she gave birth to her firstborn son and
wrapped him in bands of cloth, and laid him in a manger, because
there was no place for them in the inn.

Joy to the World

8 In that region there were shepherds living in the fields, keeping
watch over their flock by night. 9 Then an angel of the Lord stood
before them, and the glory of the Lord shone around them, and they
were terrified. 10 But the angel said to them, "Do not be afraid; for
see—I am bringing you good news of great joy for all the people:
11 to you is born this day in the city of David a Savior, who is the
Messiah, the Lord. 12 This will be a sign for you: you will find a
child wrapped in bands of cloth and lying in a manger." 13 And
suddenly there was with the angel a multitude of the heavenly host,
praising God and saying, 14 "Glory to God in the highest heaven,
and on earth peace among those whom he favors!"

Much to Ponder

[15] When the angels had left them and gone into heaven, the shepherds said to one another, "Let us go now to Bethlehem and see this thing that has taken place, which the Lord has made known to us." [16] So they went with haste and found Mary and Joseph, and the child lying in the manger. [17] When they saw this, they made known what had been told them about this child; [18] and all who heard it were amazed at what the shepherds told them. [19] But Mary treasured all these words and pondered them in her heart. [20] The shepherds returned, glorifying and praising God for all they had heard and seen, as it had been told them.

First Impression

5 minutes
Briefly mention a question you have about the reading or one thing in it that surprised, impressed, delighted, or challenged you. No discussion! Just listen to one another's reactions.

If participants have not read this section already, read it aloud. Otherwise go on to "Questions for Reflection and Discussion."

A Child Is Born

Joseph and Mary set out from Nazareth knowing that she is at term but not knowing how long they have before her time comes to deliver. And where will they be when the moment comes? They are relieved to make it to Bethlehem, but then the place where they hoped to stay is occupied, and they are shunted elsewhere. Uncertainty, hurried conversations, patience put to the test—the night is not shaping up as one of deep and dreamless sleep. In fact, by the time they settle into their makeshift quarters, the opportunity for sleeping has passed. We may picture a couple of women from the neighborhood offering to help. Things move along. Joseph waits in the darkness. After some time there comes that ever surprising sound: a tiny gulp and a startled, vigorous wail. The child is born.

"She gave birth," Luke says simply. We can picture what followed. Mary took the baby in her arms, guided him to nourishment, and whispered to him. With some help he was cleaned up and wrapped warmly. When he began to doze, someone—Joseph?—converted an empty feeding trough that happened to be at hand into a crib, and she put the baby down for the first time to sleep.

So the angel's announcement had come to pass: "You will bear a son." From the roots of her being, with every fiber stretched taut, she had brought him forth. She had fulfilled her affirmation: "Let it be with me according to your word." Now here he is! And what will his life be? But in the wonder of the moment, it is difficult to think of the future. Look at him, so peaceful, so perfect in every way.

Mary's reverie is broken by the voices of shepherds at the door. They want to see the baby. How do *they* know about him? "Angels told us!" The shepherds crowd around. If she had felt that her heart was too full to contain anything more, well, here is something more. She is amazed at the shepherds' report. Heaven and earth (what could be more earthy than these guys, who had been camping out with their sheep?) have been mobilized to praise God for the birth of her child. The angel's message to the shepherds sounds like Gabriel's announcement to her, but different also. Could it be Gabriel who spoke to these men?

Drawn to the center of God's engagement with the human race, her ears ringing with the excited words of angels and shepherds—could the new mother be anything but exhausted and overwhelmed? But that is not how Luke pictures her. As the shepherds leave, his camera zooms in on Mary, and we see her sitting quiet but alert: "Mary treasured all these words and pondered them in her heart." She cannot fathom all that God is about, yet she opens her heart wider and wider to embrace it. The young mother totally intent on the mystery of her son: this is Luke's Christmas card for us, his nativity icon.

Not What You Would Expect

Luke highlights the contradictoriness of the situation: a foreign power dominates the country into which God sends his king to his people. From distant Rome, the emperor Augustus (his name, which means "the August One," has a blasphemous ring) is so much in control of Palestine that he can set people moving from one end of the country to the other by a mere decree. His command compels Joseph and Mary to make the trip from Nazareth to Bethlehem at an inconvenient time. Yet as a result, Jesus is born in Bethlehem, the town of David, where God had promised to raise up a great ruler for his people (Micah 5:2). So who, Luke asks us, is really in control? Is it Augustus? Or God, who accomplishes his purposes without consulting earthly rulers, and even mysteriously, by letting them have their way?

No one could have been more painfully aware of the contradictoriness of the situation than Joseph and Mary. They would rather have been at home in Nazareth, no doubt. The place they got pushed aside into in Bethlehem, whatever it was (see page 53), was a less-than-ideal delivery room. It would have been easy for them to get upset with God for not providing more suitable accommodations for the arrival of his Son. Yet Mary's face at the end of the night—so peaceful and attentive to God—leaves no doubt that she, and surely Joseph also, viewed the situation with eyes of faith.

What about us? When we feel uncertain and disappointed, do we look on our situation with eyes of faith? When forces outside our control shape our lives in ways that are adverse to our welfare, do we look with trust to God who accomplishes his purposes under such conditions?

Reflections on the Reading

Like every woman who has just given birth for the first time, Mary finds herself cast up on the shore of a vast new continent— motherhood. And her motherhood enfolds the deepest mystery, God's entry into the human race: "He will be called the Son of God." Mary has much to ponder, and the vantage point of her pondering is unique. Her amazement as a new mother at the life brought forth from within her merges with amazement at the coming of God's Son. As Mary puts Jesus to the breast, love for her baby and love for her God join; the mother's nurturing care for her child and the creature's total devotion to her creator become one and the same love. Mary receives the mystery of God's entering into humanity in the divine and human person Jesus with a single worshipful and maternal love.

Although Mary's vantage point for pondering the incarnation is unique, also unique in a certain way is the point of view of Joseph and of the shepherds. They were there the night Jesus was born. Yet the good news of Jesus' birth is not that once, long ago and far away, God was born into the world and a few people had the opportunity to see him in the hours after his birth. No, at the beginning of his Gospel, Luke (1:1) tells us that he is writing about "the events that have been fulfilled among us." He regards the nativity as an event among us now, wherever we are. Each of us can join Mary in her wonder and joy at Jesus' birth, because he has come to be present in our lives and to draw us into the mystery of his coming.

Questions for Reflection and Discussion

45 minutes
Choose questions according to your interest and time.

1 Compare the description of the appearance of the angels in Luke 2:9, 13–14, with the descriptions of Gabriel's appearances in Luke 1:11 and 1:28. What is different in the appearance to the shepherds? Why this difference?

2 In what ways is the angelic announcement to the shepherds (Luke 2:10–12) similar to Gabriel's announcement to Mary (Luke 1:30–33, 35–37)? When the shepherds relayed the announcement to Mary, would doing so have added to her knowledge of her son?

3 Luke shows us that when God's Son came into the world, kings and governors were absent from the scene, but a poor couple and shepherds were present. Is there a message in this for us?

4 Luke's account of Jesus' birth in verses 1–7 illustrates the old saying, "God writes straight with crooked lines." Traveling to Bethlehem at the end of Mary's pregnancy would have been difficult for Mary and Joseph. But because of that journey, Jesus was born in Bethlehem, the city of his ancestor David.

When has God used twisting paths to bring you to a place he wanted you to be?

5 The angels announce the birth of the Savior. How have you experienced Jesus as savior?

6 The shepherds go back to their field "glorifying and praising God for all they had heard and seen." When do you praise God? What actions of God lead you to praise him? Is there some way you might praise and glorify God more than you do?

7 First, think of terms that describe what God is like—what makes God, God. Then consider how your portrayal of God fits with the idea that God became a baby. What is difficult about this picture? How does it enrich your understanding of God?

8 **Focus question.** "Mary treasured all these words and pondered them in her heart." Do you ponder God's words and deeds? What helps you to do this? What effect does it have on your life? How could doing so help you grow in treasuring God's word?

Prayer to Close

10 minutes
Use this approach—or create your own!

◆ Some prayers in the Byzantine Christmas liturgy show Mary speaking to her newborn son. Take turns praying the following excerpts, pausing after each for silent reflection. End with an Our Father and a Hail Mary.

The Virgin held him in her arms and without ceasing kissed him. Filled with joy, she said aloud, "Shall I nurse you—you who give nourishment to the world?"

"How shall I, who am your handmaiden, call you my son?"

"O Most High God, O invisible King, how is it that I look upon you?"

"I cannot understand the mystery of your limitless poverty, for the smallest of caves finds room for you within itself."

"I hold in my arms as a child you who uphold all, and I am filled with amazement. I glorify your measureless kindness toward humanity, by which you save a perishing world."

Living Tradition

A Barn or a Cave?

Our mental picture of the setting of Jesus' birth has been shaped by nativity sets, crèches. St. Francis created this image in 1223 by orchestrating a celebration of the nativity with a thatched hut and peasants. But Matthew says simply, "Jesus was born in Bethlehem" (Matthew 2:1). Luke tells us that Mary "wrapped him in swaddling clothes and laid him in a manger, because there was no room for them in the inn." (Luke 2:7). So what kind of place was Jesus born in?

When Luke writes that there was no room in the "inn," he uses a Greek word that may mean either "inn" or "guest room." Jesus uses this word when he instructs his disciples to prepare for the Last Supper. "Say to the owner of the house, 'Where is the guest room, where I may eat?'" (Luke 22:11).

In the nativity narrative, Luke may mean that there was no room at the "inn." In that case, Luke is telling us that the hotel was full, so Joseph and Mary took refuge elsewhere—perhaps in a barn, because there was a manger there. But if Luke means "guest room" here, we may picture Joseph staying with relatives in Bethlehem, in a home that had a guest room, but one that was occupied. So Joseph and Mary had to move to another part of the house. But could there have been a manger in a house? If the house was built into a hillside, it might have had a cave at the back where small animals could be sheltered. There could well have been a manger in such a back room.

So perhaps we should trade in our picture of Mary giving birth in a thatched, barnlike structure for a picture of her giving birth to Jesus in a cave at the back of a house. There is, in fact, an ancient tradition that Jesus was born in a cave. It is attested by the *Protogospel of James* (see page 11) and by Justin Martyr, a Christian writer who grew up in Palestine in the early second century.

Living Tradition
Ever a Virgin

At one point in Mark's Gospel, people in Nazareth express astonishment that Jesus is announcing God's kingdom and performing miracles. "Where did this man get all this?" they ask. "Is not this the carpenter, the son of Mary?" (Mark 6:2–3). The neighbors' amazement at Jesus' doings indicates how ordinary he had seemed to them. As he was growing up, nothing about him led them to expect that he would have a powerful, prophetic ministry. Apparently nothing about Mary seemed exceptional to them, either. How can Jesus be so extraordinary, their question implies, when his mother is just one of us?

The Nazarenes' estimate of Mary may surprise us, because we know she was an extraordinary person indeed. But there is a difference between responding deeply to God and living in an unusual way. The Gospel writers do not depict Mary as acting in a manner that would have set her outside the mainstream of her society. Luke, for example, portrays her as deeply devout—humble and obedient to God, imbued with Scripture, attentive to God's action in her life—but devout according to the Judaism of her day. From her neighbors' opinion of her, we may conclude that she lived in Nazareth pretty much in the way a respectable wife and mother was expected to live.

Making Adjustments

Yet if Mary and Joseph were in many ways a regular couple in their society, they confronted an utterly unique situation: their child, whom Mary had virginally conceived by the Holy Spirit, was the Son of God. Taking account of this awesome reality, they departed at times from the usual ways of doing things. In their day, a devout Jewish man would break off the engagement if his betrothed was discovered to have become pregnant before they came together. But Joseph, instructed by an angel, did not let Mary's pregnancy derail their wedding plans (see Matthew 1:18–24). As we will see in the next reading, Mary and Joseph deviated from the usual manner of fulfilling a precept of the Mosaic law about firstborn sons because of their son's special status.

Generally following accepted customs but making adjustments in light of the great, new thing that God was doing with them—this was the approach that the holy couple also took to their marriage. Nothing in the Gospels leads us to doubt that they conducted their married life according to the expectations of their time. And, given the depth of their relationship with God, they must have had a deep love for each other. But because of their unique situation, they departed from the usual pattern at an important point: they decided never to have marital relations.

Why a Virgin?

It is easier to say why Mary and Joseph reached this decision than when or how. For Mary, it was a matter of total dedication to God. As Pope John Paul II put it, God guided Mary to accept her vocation to be the mother of the Son of God with a "spousal love." In other words, by her "may it be done to me according to your word" she made a total consecration of herself to God—the kind that a woman makes to her husband. Mary felt called not merely to fulfill the biological and social role of mother but to make a gift of her whole self in love to God, who was favoring her with this incomprehensible blessing. "By virtue of this love," John Paul writes, "Mary wished to be always and in all things 'given to God,' living in virginity. The words 'Behold, I am the handmaid of the Lord' express the fact that from the outset she accepted and understood her own motherhood as a total gift of self, a gift of her person to the service of the saving plans of the Most High." For Mary, then, virginity was essential for expressing her response to God.

On Joseph's side, respect for Mary's virginity was a way of showing reverence for God's unique call to her, God's incarnate presence in her and through her. Although Mary belonged to Joseph as his wife, she belonged in a prior and absolute way to God. Out of genuine love for her, Joseph appreciated and supported that sacred relationship.

Mary may have made the decision to remain a virgin before her engagement to Joseph. Many readers have detected such a commitment in her words to the angel—"I am a virgin" (Luke 1:34)—understanding this statement as a declaration about herself past, present, and future. It is impossible, however, to be certain that Mary decided on this course of action before her betrothal. Such a plan would have been unprecedented in the culture of the time, and the evangelists do not positively indicate it. Another possibility is that, after Gabriel's announcement, Mary and Joseph together reached the decision to refrain from sexual relations because of her desire to give herself to God as fully as possible in response to his revelation of his plans for her.

Whenever it was that they made this decision, for Mary it meant a life that was extraordinary within the ordinary. She lived in a relationship of virginal dedication to God in the context of a loving marriage and in the midst of the household work, farm chores, and relations with relatives and neighbors that filled a married woman's days in Nazareth.

Later, during his ministry, Jesus opened up consecrated virginity as a way of life for disciples gifted to embrace it. This life consecrated totally to God bears witness that the kingdom of God is so real and has come so close that a person can live for it and in it in this radical way even in the present world (Matthew 19:11–12). Those who knew Mary well might have regarded her as, in a sense, Jesus' first disciple—totally dedicated to her son and his mission. Little did they know that she was also the first of his disciples to embrace virginity as an expression of total love and commitment to him.

Perpetual Virginity

Although the evangelists highlight Mary's virginal conception of Jesus, her life-long virginity is not explicitly presented in the gospels. Our knowledge of it comes from a hidden stream of tradition in the earliest Christian community—a stream that flowed beneath the surface for some time and came into the open only after the Gospels were written. Beginning in the second century, the conviction that Mary remained a virgin is attested to in Christian writings. By the fourth century, we know of numerous Christian teachers who accepted her perpetual virginity as a part of the tradition they had received from the apostles. Ultimately, it is the Church's affirmation of this belief that is the seal of its authenticity. The Holy Spirit guided the people of God to affirm and appreciate this aspect of Mary's life.

Some statements in the New Testament have seemed to some readers to conflict with the picture of Mary as lifelong virgin. It may be helpful to say a few words about those statements.

"[He] had no relations with her *until* she had borne a son" (Matthew 1:25). The *until* suggests that Joseph might have had sexual relations with Mary after Jesus was born. Although this seems a reasonable inference from the statement in English, it is not the implication of the Greek in which Matthew wrote. The Greek word translated as *until* does not imply that a change takes place after the "until" event occurs. For example, Matthew quotes this prophecy about Jesus: "He will not break a bruised reed or quench a smoldering wick until he brings justice to victory" (Matthew 12:20). The prophecy did not mean to suggest that once Jesus brought justice to victory he would begin bruising reeds and quenching smoldering wicks. Matthew quotes Jesus declaring: "There are some standing here who will not taste death until they see the Son of Man coming in his kingdom" (Matthew 16:28, *NAB*). Obviously, Jesus was not implying that some would taste death *after* the Son of Man comes. Thus, Matthew's statement about Joseph and Mary refraining from sexual relations until Jesus was born does not indicate anything about their behavior after that. Matthew's point was to underline the fact that Mary conceived Jesus not by Joseph but by the Holy Spirit.

"She gave birth to her firstborn son" (Luke 2:7). This statement might seem to imply that later Mary bore other children. But in Jewish culture, *firstborn* was not merely a birth-order designation; it was a legal term, indicating rights of inheritance and authority in the family. Thus, *firstborn* could be applied to a woman's first child before any siblings came along, and even if no siblings came along. This is illustrated by the tombstone of a Jewish woman from 5 B.C. that indicates that she died while giving birth "to a firstborn child."

Jesus' "Brothers"

"Is this not the carpenter, the son of Mary and brother of James and Joses and Judas and Simon, and are not his sisters here with us?"

(Mark 6:3; for other references to Jesus' "brothers," see Mark 3:31–35; John 7:3; Acts 1:14, 12:17, 15:13, and 21:18; 1 Corinthians 15:7; Galatians 1:19; 2:9, 12). In English this question from the townspeople of Nazareth implies that Mary had more children than Jesus. Even the Greek of Matthew's Gospel might at first seem to carry this implication. But there is a further language issue here. Behind the evangelist's Greek is the Aramaic spoken in Palestine in Jesus' day. And the Aramaic word for *brother*—like the corresponding Hebrew word—is more inclusive than the English word for *brother*. The Aramaic and Hebrew words for *brother* mean "close male relative"; they can refer to a full sibling, a half brother, a stepbrother, an uncle, a nephew, a cousin. In fact, Aramaic and Hebrew did not have distinct words for these relationships. If you needed to specify that a man called a brother was actually a cousin, you would say something like "he is my father's sister's son." When it wasn't necessary to be so specific, you would just say, "He's my brother." Thus, for example, the Hebrew word for *brother* is applied to nephews in Genesis 24:48 and 29:12 and to cousins in Leviticus 10:4 and 1 Chronicles 23:22.

Greek did have distinct words for cousin and nephew and so on. But Mark followed Aramaic and Hebrew biblical usage, rather than a more specific Greek term, when he referred to a ruler named Philip as the "brother" of Herod Antipas, ruler of Galilee. Mark surely knew that they were actually half brothers (Mark 6:17–18).

The upshot of this is that in the Hebrew and Aramaic portions of the Old Testament, and even in the Greek New Testament, from the term *brother* alone—likewise *sister* alone—we cannot know the exact nature of the relationship between family members. *Brother* and *sister* may mean sibling, but then again, they may not, and without further information, we cannot know for sure. Thus, the brothers and sisters of Jesus referred to in the New Testament were not necessarily his full siblings.

If these brothers and sisters were not children of Mary, what relationship did they have to Jesus? The two main theories have been that they were children of Joseph by a previous marriage, Joseph having been widowed before marrying Mary, or that they were cousins. Both views have ancient support. The Greek-speaking Church Fathers Origen (who died in 254) and Epiphanius (who died in 403) attested to the tradition that the brothers of the Lord were sons of Joseph by an earlier marriage. The Latin-speaking Church Father Jerome (who died in 420) interpreted the brothers and sisters of Jesus as cousins and regarded Joseph as a celibate. The cousins view has prevailed in the Western Church; Eastern Christians maintain the stepbrothers and stepsisters view.

Whether we think of James and Joses and the rest as stepsiblings or cousins of Jesus, they are a reminder to us of the family dimension of Mary's life. Families were dense and extensive in the ancient world. Mary was not only wife and mother, but also, perhaps, stepmother, and almost certainly niece, cousin, second cousin, third cousin, sister-in-law, aunt, and so on. Although she expressed her total dedication to God by remaining a virgin, she lived out her calling not in the isolation of a cloister or a cave but in the midst of a life crowded with other people, many of whom had a claim on her attention as members of her extended family.

Virgin full of grace,
I know that at Nazareth you lived modestly,
without requesting anything more.
Neither ecstasies, nor miracles, nor other extra ordinary deeds
enhanced your life, O Queen of the elect.
The number of the lowly, "the little ones," is very great on earth.
They can raise their eyes to your without any fear.
You are the incomparable Mother
who walk with them along the common way to guide them to heaven.
Beloved Mother, in this harsh exile,
I want to live always with you
and follow you every day.
All my fears vanish under your motherly gaze
which teaches me to weep and to rejoice! Amen.

St. Thérèse of Lisieux

SURPRISED IN THE TEMPLE

Questions to Begin

10 minutes
Use a question or two to get warmed up for the reading.

---

1 How did your parents choose your name?

---

2 As a child, did you ever get lost? Or, as a parent, did you ever lose a child?

Almighty ever-living God,
we humbly implore your majesty
that, just as your Only Begotten Son
was presented on this day in the Temple
in the substance of our flesh,
so, by your grace,
we may be presented to you with minds made pure.

Collect prayer, Mass for the Presentation of the Lord

10 minutes
*Read the passage aloud. Let individuals take turns
reading paragraphs.*

The Reading: Luke 2:21–52

The Baby Is Circumcised and Named

2:21 After eight days had passed, it was time to circumcise the child;
and he was called Jesus, the name given by the angel before he was
conceived in the womb.

Ritual Purification and Presentation in the Temple

22 When the time came for their purification according to the law of
Moses, they brought him up to Jerusalem to present him to the Lord
23 (as it is written in the law of the Lord, "Every firstborn male shall
be designated as holy to the Lord"), 24 and they offered a sacrifice
according to what is stated in the law of the Lord, "a pair of turtle-
doves or two young pigeons."

An Unexpected Encounter

25 Now there was a man in Jerusalem whose name was Simeon; this man
was righteous and devout, looking forward to the consolation of Israel,
and the Holy Spirit rested on him. 26 It had been revealed to him by the
Holy Spirit that he would not see death before he had seen the Lord's
Messiah. 27 Guided by the Spirit, Simeon came into the temple; and when
the parents brought in the child Jesus, to do for him what was customary
under the law, 28 Simeon took him in his arms and praised God, saying,
> 29 "Master, now you are dismissing your servant in peace,
>   according to your word;
> 30 for my eyes have seen your salvation,
> 31 which you have prepared in the presence of all peoples,
> 32 a light for revelation to the Gentiles
>   and for glory to your people Israel."

33 And the child's father and mother were amazed at what was
being said about him. 34 Then Simeon blessed them and said to his
mother Mary, "This child is destined for the falling and the rising of
many in Israel, and to be a sign that will be opposed 35 so that the
inner thoughts of many will be revealed—and a sword will pierce
your own soul too."

A Prophet Spreads Good News

36 There was also a prophet, Anna the daughter of Phanuel, of the
tribe of Asher. She was of a great age, having lived with her husband
for seven years after her marriage, 37 then as a widow to the age

of eighty-four. She never left the temple but worshipped there with fasting and prayer night and day. 38 At that moment she came, and began to praise God and to speak about the child to all who were looking for the redemption of Jerusalem.

The Hidden Life

39 When they had finished everything required by the law of the Lord, they returned to Galilee, to their own town of Nazareth. 40 The child grew and became strong, filled with wisdom; and the favor of God was upon him.

An Unexpected Absence

41 Now every year his parents went to Jerusalem for the festival of the Passover. 42 And when he was twelve years old, they went up as usual for the festival. 43 When the festival was ended and they started to return, the boy Jesus stayed behind in Jerusalem, but his parents did not know it. 44 Assuming that he was in the group of travelers, they went a day's journey. Then they started to look for him among their relatives and friends. 45 When they did not find him, they returned to Jerusalem to search for him.

A Confrontation in the Temple

46 After three days they found him in the temple, sitting among the teachers, listening to them and asking them questions. 47 And all who heard him were amazed at his understanding and his answers. 48 When his parents saw him they were astonished; and his mother said to him, "Child, why have you treated us like this? Look, your father and I have been searching for you in great anxiety." 49 He said to them, "Why were you searching for me? Did you not know that I must be in my Father's house?" 50 But they did not understand what he said to them.

51 Then he went down with them and came to Nazareth, and was obedient to them. His mother treasured all these things in her heart. 52 And Jesus increased in wisdom and in years, and in divine and human favor.

First Impression

5 minutes
Briefly mention a question you have about the reading or one thing in it that surprised, impressed, delighted, or challenged you. No discussion! Just listen to one another's reactions.

If participants have not read this section already, read it aloud. Otherwise go on to "Questions for Reflection and Discussion."

What Were They Doing in the Temple?

Luke 2:22–38. After childbirth, according to the Mosaic law, the mother needs to be ritually purified. In Mary's time, this involved sacrificing a lamb. If that sacrifice was a financial burden, the family could substitute a few inexpensive birds (Leviticus 12:8). Perhaps regretfully, Joseph and Mary had to take the cheaper option.

Under the Mosaic law, the baby did not need ritual purification. But by birth order and gender, every firstborn boy belonged to God in a special way. Moses had stated that "every firstborn male shall be designated as holy to the Lord" (2:23), meaning "set apart for God." If the boy was to grow up in ordinary life, he had to be released from that special status. The release was called "redemption": the boy was, so to speak, bought back from God. Redemption was a simple matter: a monetary payment to a priest a month after the birth. The payment could be made anywhere; a trip to the temple was not required. Joseph and Mary, however, make a point of going to the temple—and then they do not follow the practice of redeeming the boy. Instead, they "present him to the Lord" (2:22)—something for which there was no Jewish tradition. What are they thinking?

Luke tells us that Mary and Joseph "do for him what was customary under the law." Another translation would be "do the custom of the law *in regard to him*," in other words, to do what the law prescribed for him in particular. Remembering Gabriel's words that "the child to be born will be holy" (Luke 1:35), Mary and Joseph realize that the dictum "every firstborn male is holy" pertains to Jesus in a unique way. He is holy, that is, he belongs to God, absolutely. After considering the matter, Mary and Joseph conclude that the law calls for something special in his case. Perhaps guided by the command to "set apart to the LORD all that first opens the womb" (Exodus 13:12), they bring Jesus to the temple and present him to God, in effect saying, "Dear God, here is your Son. He does indeed belong entirely to you."

By omitting the usual redemption of the boy, Mary and Joseph signify that Jesus is not withdrawn from the status of total dedication to God. Jesus will grow up as a layman, not as a priest in the temple, but he will be entirely devoted to God throughout his life.

Thus, Joseph and Mary demonstrate an ability to interpret what Scripture says regarding Jesus. Later Jesus will interpret for his disciples the things "about himself" in Scripture (Luke 24:27). Here his parents show that they already have a gift for penetrating what the Scriptures say about him.

Simeon's Role

Because there was no prescribed ritual for presenting a baby in the temple, we may wonder how exactly Joseph and Mary planned to go about it. Whatever they had in mind, the Spirit takes charge of the situation, steering Simeon in their direction. By putting Jesus in the arms of this devout man, his parents express his presentation to God.

Discerning though they are, the couple's encounter with Simeon suggests the limits of their understanding of God's plans. When the old man speaks of Jesus' role, Joseph and Mary are taken aback. It is not Simeon's words about "glory to your people Israel"; those words echo Mary's own prayer celebrating God's coming to save the Jewish people (Luke 1:54–55). But Mary and Joseph do not expect to hear that through their child God will manifest his glory to *all* peoples. They must notice, too, that Simeon speaks of God's revelation to the gentiles first, before mentioning Israel. Hearing Israel put in second position must come as a surprise to them. Perhaps Simeon himself is surprised by the words he is inspired to utter, as he has spent a lifetime waiting for "the consolation of Israel."

"A Sword Will Pierce Your Soul"

"This child is destined for the fall and rise of many"—Simeon confirms Mary's conviction that God will bring down the mighty and raise up the lowly. But there is a disturbing note. Her son will encounter opposition. As conflict arises, people's motivations will be exposed, and some will be ugly. "A sword will pierce your own soul," Simeon tells Mary. Quick-witted and discerning as she is, Mary may already feel the sword's tip. Simeon has implied that she may have to detach herself from her expectations of national restoration. Later Jesus will make it plain to his disciples that he has not come to restore the Jewish people to independence in their land but to liberate the whole world from forms of oppression deeper than those imposed by the Romans. The disciples will not find this word easy to accept. Will Mary?

Mary's deepest suffering will stem from her love for her son. Eventually, Jesus will leave Nazareth to carry out his mission, and Mary, keenly aware of his vulnerability, will have to let him go. In the end, she will lose him to a cruel death—although that pain is probably not uppermost in Luke's mind here, because he does not mention Mary's presence at the cross.

Anna: The First Evangelist

Luke 2:36–38. Simeon has spoken only to Mary and Joseph. But a very elderly woman named Anna now appears—she is somewhere between her mid-eighties and mid-hundreds—and, guided by the Spirit, she begins to tell people in the temple courtyard about Jesus. Thus, Anna is the first evangelist in Luke's Gospel (it is interesting that in John's Gospel, two women are early evangelists: an unnamed woman in Samaria and Mary Magdalene). Notice the mind-set of those to whom Anna speaks: they are "looking for the redemption of Jerusalem." The one they have been expecting has indeed come. He will disappoint their expectations by transcending them.

A Sharp Exchange

Luke 2:39–52. Mary and Joseph do not seem to have been overprotective parents. At least, they didn't require Jesus to check in with them every hour throughout the day. But his disappearance throws them into a panic. Is he hurt? In trouble?

Back at the temple, Jesus is asking questions and giving answers—not just seeking and supplying information but also posing challenging questions and demonstrating an ability to handle them. After a couple of days of this, the learned men invite Jesus to sit with them as an equal. Any surprise Mary and Joseph might feel when they come upon this display of precocity is overshadowed by their shock at his irresponsible behavior. He hasn't been injured or kidnapped; he simply decided to stay behind and failed to let them know! "We've been tormented over you," Mary reproaches him. Her question is not "Why are you here?" but "Why did you do this to us?"

Jesus' response can be translated as "I had to be in my Father's house" or "about my Father's business" or even "among my Father's people," that is, among those who teach God's law. Whatever the nuance, it is a pretty sharp way for a twelve-year-old to speak to his parents in public (the *you* is plural). Perhaps there is an implied reproach in his words: "Remember how, rather than redeeming me, you presented me to God right here in the temple, as a sign that I belong to him? So where else did you expect me to be than here, in his house, inquiring into his law?" Jesus challenges his mother and foster father to set aside their own interests and conform themselves to God's purposes. Simeon's prophecy to Mary is being fulfilled. A sword of division pierces her heart—the division between her expectations and God's purposes for his Son.

This is the only conversation between Mary and Jesus in Luke's Gospel. Does Luke intend it to represent other conversations between them over the years?

Back in Nazareth, Jesus will continue to be about his Father's business. For some twenty years, his Father's business will involve obeying his parents, farming, doing construction work—the typical life of a young man in a Galilean village.

Reflections on the Readings

Mary's conversation with Jesus is at least the fourth time we see her being surprised (compare Luke 1:29; 2:18–19, 33). If Mary was a peaceful woman, it wasn't because she had life figured out from the get-go. Her peace lay in knowing that her life was in God's hands, but he was revealing his plans only one step at a time, and some steps were not what she expected. She needed to trust God as much as any of us needs to do.

Nevertheless, Luke does not depict Mary as a pawn in a divine chess game. Her first and last words in Luke's Gospel are questions. Mary "treasured all these things in her heart": she sought to penetrate the saving plan that God was unfolding, so that she could understand it and play her part in it to the full.

Questions for Reflection and Discussion

45 minutes
Choose questions according to your interest and time.

1 Artists usually depict Simeon as an old man. Is there a basis for that in the text of Luke's Gospel? Anna is explicitly said to be old. Why does Luke give us this information? What difference does it make for understanding the episode?

2 What Jewish religious laws and customs does Luke show Joseph and Mary observing in this reading? What do those observances tell us about the holy couple?

3 What role does the Holy Spirit play in the episodes of our reading this week? What role in episodes in previous weeks? What impression of the Spirit do you get from all of these episodes? What does this suggest to you about how and where the Spirit wants to be active in people's lives? In your life?

4 Simeon experienced the greatest moment of fulfillment in his life when he held Jesus in his arms (verses 29–30). When have you experienced a moment of fulfillment? What kind of fulfillment do you want to experience?

5   Simeon's words to God, "Now you are dismissing your servant in peace" (verse 29), could also be translated as "You may let your servant depart in peace." Simeon feels that he can die in peace. What do you think is needed for a person to die in peace? Are you ready to die in peace?

6   Knowing that Jesus is God's Son, how can Luke say of him that he grew in strength and wisdom (verses 40 and 52)?

7   What does it mean to present oneself to the Lord? How do you present yourself to the Lord? How might you grow in doing this?

8   **Focus question.** What is the "business" the Father is giving you at this time in your life? How might Jesus' example in this week's reading (verses 41–52) guide you in carrying it out?

Prayer to Close

10 minutes
Use this approach—or create your own!

One of the best-known prayers to Mary is the Memorare (Latin for "Remember!"), by St. Bernard of Clairvaux. Pray it together, then follow with spontaneous prayers for your own needs and those of others.

◆ Remember, O most loving Virgin Mary, that never was it known that anyone who fled to your protection, implored your help, or sought your intercession was left unaided. Inspired by this confidence, we fly unto you, O virgin of virgins, our mother. To you we come, before you we stand, sinful and sorrowful. O mother of the Word incarnate, despise not our petitions, but in your mercy hear and answer us.

A Request at a Wedding

Questions to Begin

10 minutes
Use a question or two to get warmed up for the reading.

1 What is your favorite part of wedding celebrations?

2 What improvements would you suggest for how weddings are celebrated?

"Our mother the Virgin . . . shows us Jesus as the Master of the truth whom we must listen to and follow: 'Do whatever he tells you.' Mary continually repeats this word wherever she carries her son in her arms and points him out with her glance."

Blessed John Paul II, at the Sanctuary of Our Lady of Suyapa, Honduras, 1983

10 minutes
Read the passage aloud. Let individuals take turns
reading paragraphs.

The Background

Jesus has not yet launched his public ministry, but he has begun to gather disciples. These first disciples accompany him to Cana, a village just a few miles from Nazareth.

The Reading: John 2:1–12

Time for Good Wine

2:1 There was a wedding in Cana of Galilee, and the mother of Jesus was there. 2 Jesus and his disciples had also been invited to the wedding. 3 When the wine gave out, the mother of Jesus said to him, "They have no wine." 4 And Jesus said to her, "Woman, what concern is that to you and to me? My hour has not yet come." 5 His mother said to the servants, "Do whatever he tells you." 6 Now standing there were six stone water-jars for the Jewish rites of purification, each holding twenty or thirty gallons. 7 Jesus said to them, "Fill the jars with water." And they filled them up to the brim. 8 He said to them, "Now draw some out, and take it to the chief steward." So they took it. 9 When the steward tasted the water that had become wine, and did not know where it came from (though the servants who had drawn the water knew), the steward called the bridegroom 10 and said to him, "Everyone serves the good wine first, and then the inferior wine after the guests have become drunk. But you have kept the good wine until now." 11 Jesus did this, the first of his signs, in Cana of Galilee, and revealed his glory; and his disciples believed in him.

Jesus Begins His Public Ministry

12 After this he went down to Capernaum with his mother, his brothers, and his disciples; and they remained there a few days.

First Impression

5 minutes
Briefly mention a question you have about the reading or one thing in it that surprised, impressed, delighted, or challenged you. No discussion! Just listen to one another's reactions.

Exploring the Theme

If participants have not read this section already, read it aloud. Otherwise go on to "Questions for Reflection and Discussion."

Mary Takes Charge

John 2:1–11. Like Nazareth, Cana was a small town. Archaeologists estimate that only about five hundred people lived there. But a wedding celebration there might last a week. If everybody showed up and stayed on, the host could easily run out of wine.

Mary seems to have been more than a guest at the wedding. John does not say that she was invited but simply that she "was there." And when a need arose, she knew about it and took charge of the situation, and she was in a position to give directions to the servants. We might suspect that Mary was often in this house. Presumably, it was the home of some relatives or close friends. We seem to get a glimpse here of Mary's social life.

What did Mary expect Jesus to do? He may never have performed a miracle before this moment. People in Nazareth, at least, did not know of his working any miracles during the years he lived in their town (see Mark 6:1–3). But, as the New Testament scholar F. F. Bruce remarks, Mary "knew that in such a crisis she could not do better than call upon her Son's resourcefulness. Probably she had learned by experience that to draw his attention to a need was a sure way of getting something done."

Jesus, however, declines to get involved. He does it politely, addressing Mary as "woman"—his usual way of speaking to women in public (Matthew 15:28; Luke 13:12; John 4:21, 8:10, 20:13). But his question—"What concern is that to you and to me?"—is a way of saying, "It's none of my business." He adds an enigmatic statement: "My hour has not yet come." Jesus' "hour" is his return to his Father by death and resurrection (John 7:30; 8:20; 12:23, 27; 13:1; 17:1). The timing of his hour lies entirely with the Father (see Mark 14:35; John 12:27). Jesus' point, it seems, is that his attention is focused on his Father's agenda for him, not on doing favors for his family. Later he will make a similar point to some of his male relatives (John 7:3–6).

Jesus' words constitute a gentle no, but Mary acts as though he had said yes. Feeling no need to persist in seeking his help, she turns to the servants and tells them to follow whatever instructions he gives them. Not only is she confident he will take

action; she seems to know that his action will involve them.
By speaking of his hour, Jesus has reminded his mother of his
relationship with his heavenly Father—a relationship that remains a
mystery even to her. Yet her instruction to the servants shows that
she has an insight into Jesus' thinking. She can read her son.

A Ray of Glory

Jesus turns roughly 150 gallons of water into wine—surely enough
for a celebration in Cana! In this act, his disciples see his "glory."
Jesus' glory lies in his relationship with the Father. It will be revealed
when he glorifies the Father by laying down his life in obedient love
and when the Father glorifies him by raising him in triumph over
death. In Cana, Jesus has let a ray of that divine glory shine out, at
his mother's request.

     With this revelation of his glory, Jesus' disciples "believed
in him"—or, at least, begin to believe in him, for they will not
attain full belief in Jesus until he rises from the dead. In fact, their
progress from unbelief to belief is part of the drama of John's
Gospel. The climax is Thomas's recognition of Jesus' identity: "My
Lord and my God!" (John 20:28). Notice, however, that John does
not say here that Mary came to believe in Jesus. Jesus' miracle
did not bring her to faith; rather, her faith evoked the miracle. Even
before Jesus begins his ministry, his mother believes in him. She
is the first of those he praises at the end: "Blessed are those who
have not seen and yet have come to believe" (John 20:29).

Reflections on the Reading

The Gospels recount only two conversations between Mary and Jesus—
as he enters adulthood and as he begins his ministry (Luke 2:48–51;
John 2:3–4). Despite differences between them, the conversations are
strikingly similar. Mary begins by expressing her view of the situation;
Jesus responds by emphasizing the primacy of his relationship with his
Father. This distances him from his mother, but then he then acts in a
way that confirms his closeness to her. The two conversations give us
an insight into their relationship.

Questions for Reflection and Discussion

45 minutes
Choose questions according to your interest and time.

1 Reread verse 3. Why do you think Mary doesn't ask Jesus directly to take care of the problem with the wine?

2 Why do you suppose Jesus doesn't simply tell his mother that he will take care of the problem?

3 John often quotes people saying more than they realize. How might this be true of the bridegroom's words in verse 10?

4 Jesus' disciples saw his glory (verse 11). What does it mean to see Jesus' glory? When have you seen Jesus' glory? How has this affected you?

5 Jesus' disciples believed in him (verse 11). What does it mean to believe in Jesus?

6 What might be the significance of Jesus giving his disciples the first revelation of his glory at a wedding?

7 How aware are you of the needs of people around you? How can a person grow in this kind of awareness?

8 **Focus question.** Mary tells the servants, "Do whatever he tells you." Has there been a particular situation in your life when you took this instruction as your guide? How did things turn out? What effect did this have on you? Mary's words are an invitation to listen to Jesus. How can a person do that? What does Mary's instruction mean for you at this present time?

Prayer to Close

10 minutes
Use this approach—or create your own!

◆ Let one person pray the requests and the group respond. Then let individuals add any further petitions. End with a Hail Mary.

Leader: Let us pray for all those who lack the basic necessities of life.

Response: Lord Jesus Christ, you turned water into wine at Cana. Have mercy on us!

Leader: Let us pray for all who long to glimpse the glory of God. *Response [as above]*.

Leader: Let us pray for ourselves as disciples of Jesus, that we might grow in faith in him. *Response [as above]*.

Leader: Let us pray that we would be attentive to everything that he tells us to do. *Response [as above]*.

Leader: Let us pray that God would make us attentive to the needs of people around us. *Response [as above]*.

Leader: Let us pray that Jesus would visit our homes with his presence and love. *Response [as above]*.

Saint in the Making

Conflict in the Family

A s soon as Jesus launched his public mission, large numbers of people started coming to him wherever he went, wanting to hear him speak and to be healed by him (Mark 2:4, 13). On one occasion when he was preaching along the shore of the Sea of Galilee, he took to a boat and spoke from out on the water so that the whole crowd could hear him—and so that he would not be crushed (Mark 3:9). The crowding became so severe that sometimes Jesus avoided entering towns and stayed out in the open countryside (Mark 1:45).

The Family Is Not Pleased

But not everyone was pleased by Jesus' activities. Opposition quickly emerged among religious leaders (Mark 2:1—3:6). It also arose closer to home. Not even his own family believed in him (John 7:3–7). And it is in an episode involving Jesus' skeptical family that we catch the only glimpse of Mary in the Gospels between the beginning of his ministry and his death.

As the scene opens, Jesus is at Peter's house in Capernaum, and a constant stream of visitors is making normal life impossible. Apparently people are crowding into the central courtyard of the house, where food is being cooked, for Mark tells us that Peter and his guests cannot even get a meal (Mark 3:19–35).

Back in Nazareth, Jesus' family has heard reports that he has become mentally unbalanced. When they learn that he has paused in his travels and is staying in Capernaum—two days' walk from Nazareth—some of them set out to take custody of him. Presumably, they plan to bring him home and force some rest on him until he returns to normal. When they arrive at Peter's house, however, they cannot get to Jesus because of a crowd around the house. When Jesus hears that they are outside, he declines to invite them in. Instead, he takes their arrival as an opportunity to declare that his *real* family members are those who commit themselves to doing God's will. Presumably, a meeting between Jesus and his relatives occurred after the crowd thinned out. But they returned to Nazareth without him.

A Mother's Worry

Mark tells us that Mary was part of the family group that went to get Jesus (Mark 3:21). Because this is the only scene in which Mary appears in Mark' Gospel, he is obviously unconcerned about giving us a portrait of her. Thus, we should be cautious in drawing conclusions about why she went along with the "brothers" to Capernaum (on Jesus' "brothers," see pages 57–59). It is impossible to picture the Mary we see at Cana—so sensitively attuned to her son— accepting a rumor that her son has become mentally ill. But did she, nevertheless, think that a little rest and home cooking would do him some good? Did she hope to soften what was shaping up to be a painful confrontation between him and the brothers? Or did she go along with the brothers simply because it would give her a chance to see him?

Although we cannot be sure of Mary's reasons for accompanying the male relatives to Capernaum, we can be fairly certain that she found the whole situation distressing. Garbled reports filtering into Nazareth about her son's tumultuous life would have given her grave concern for his well-being. And the reaction of family members to the reports must have saddened her. Family bonds were tight. We may well suppose that Mary, like any woman of her time, felt very much a part of her extended family. Undoubtedly, she loved them all. How painful for her to see them coming into conflict with her son.

Years before, when Mary and Joseph presented Jesus in the temple, Simeon had predicted that the child would become "a sign that will be opposed" (Luke 2:34). Did Mary imagine then that contradictions against him would arise even within the family? Simeon also told her that a sword would pierce her heart. The imagery summons up a situation in which hard choices have to be made, in which people have to take a stand one way or another, and the stands they take tear them apart, like a sword ripping a cloak in two. Within the family, Mary now experiences this tearing apart, as relatives take a stand against her son, and she finds herself on the other side from them, with Jesus.

Angry Neighbors

Even though the evangelists do not mention her, there is at least one other incident during Jesus' ministry from which we can be fairly sure that Mary was present. It, too, involves conflict: Jesus' visit to his home town of Nazareth.

The way Matthew (13:54–58) and Mark (6:1–6) tell it, people in Nazareth reject Jesus because his claim to be authorized by God seems at odds with what they know of him. How, they demand, could an ordinary fellow villager become a great prophet, preacher, and miracle worker? According to Luke's (4:16–30) description, people in Nazareth are willing to welcome Jesus at first, perhaps because his sudden prominence reflects positively on his town. They are proud of him. But they turn hostile when he indicates that his ministry is not geared to especially benefiting his hometown, which seems to imply also that he is not planning to especially benefit the Jewish people by bringing about a national political restoration.

In Mark's (6:4) account, Jesus remarks that a prophet should not expect to be honored in his hometown, among his relatives, and in his own extended family. This statement leads to the conclusion that not only neighbors in Nazareth but also members of his own family repudiated him.

If the visit to Capernaum with the skeptical male relatives was painful for Mary, the reaction against him in Nazareth must have been excruciating. Here were the people with whom she had lived her whole life, people who knew Jesus, who should be loyal to him, turning against him. We can only imagine the pain she felt on his behalf, watching acquaintances, friends, and family rejecting him—and her pain on behalf of those who were rejecting him: how sad to see them cutting themselves off from Jesus.

Luke tells us that, in the end, people in Nazareth actually tried to kill Jesus. They tried to drag him to a cliff and throw him off. Jesus, mysteriously, walked away from them. But the sight of neighbors and relatives turning into a mob and attacking her son would not be something Mary could ever forget. Their murderous rage must have indicated clearly to her where events in Jesus' life were headed.

The Death of Her Son

Questions to Begin

10 minutes
Use a question or two to get warmed up for the reading.

1 In hard times, whose presence have you especially appreciated?

2 Have you ever introduced two people to each other who then became good friends?

Father,
O God, who willed
that, when your Son was lifted high on the Cross,
his Mother should stand close by and share his suffering,
grant that your Church,
participating with the Virgin Mary in the Passion of Christ,
may merit a share in his Resurrection.

Collect prayer, Mass of Our Lady of Sorrows

10 minutes
Read the passage aloud. Let individuals take turns
reading paragraphs.

The Background

The wedding celebration at Cana and Jesus' crucifixion are the only two scenes in which Mary appears in John's Gospel. John indicates that there is a connection between the two events; for example, at Cana, Jesus makes a veiled reference to his death ("my hour") and addresses his mother in both scenes in the same way ("woman"). What other connections between the two episodes can you detect? What is John trying to show us by setting Cana and Golgotha side by side in this way?

The Reading: John 19:16–30

Jesus Is Crucified

19:16 So they took Jesus; 17 and carrying the cross by himself, he went out to what is called The Place of the Skull, which in Hebrew is called Golgotha. 18 There they crucified him, and with him two others, one on either side, with Jesus between them. 19 Pilate also had an inscription written and put on the cross. It read, "Jesus of Nazareth, the King of the Jews." 20 Many of the Jews read this inscription, because the place where Jesus was crucified was near the city; and it was written in Hebrew, in Latin, and in Greek. 21 Then the chief priests of the Jews said to Pilate, "Do not write, 'The King of the Jews,' but, 'This man said, I am King of the Jews.' "22 Pilate answered, "What I have written I have written."

His Clothes Are Divided Up

23 When the soldiers had crucified Jesus, they took his clothes and divided them into four parts, one for each soldier. They also took his tunic; now the tunic was seamless, woven in one piece from the top. 24 So they said to one another, "Let us not tear it, but cast lots for it to see who will get it." This was to fulfill what the scripture says, "They divided my clothes among themselves, and for my clothing they cast lots." 25 And that is what the soldiers did.

He Brings His Mother and Beloved Disciple Together

Meanwhile, standing near the cross of Jesus were his mother, and his mother's sister, Mary the wife of Clopas, and Mary Magdalene. 26 When Jesus saw his mother and the disciple whom he loved standing beside her, he said to his mother, "Woman, here is your son." 27 Then he said to the disciple, "Here is your mother." And from that hour the disciple took her into his own home.

He Breathes His Last

28 After this, when Jesus knew that all was now finished, he said (in order to fulfill the scripture), "I am thirsty." 29 A jar full of sour wine was standing there. So they put a sponge full of the wine on a branch of hyssop and held it to his mouth. 30 When Jesus had received the wine, he said, "It is finished." Then he bowed his head and gave up his spirit.

First Impression

5 minutes
Briefly mention a question you have about the reading or one thing in it that surprised, impressed, delighted, or challenged you. No discussion! Just listen to one another's reactions.

If participants have not read this section already, read it aloud.
Otherwise go on to "Questions for Reflection and Discussion."

Jesus' Hour Has Come

John 19:16–25. The four soldiers of the execution squad place
the horizontal beam of the cross on Jesus' shoulders and lead
him out from Pontius Pilate's tribunal to Golgotha, an abandoned
stone quarry just outside the city, where vertical posts were set
permanently in the rock. It is a distance of about a quarter of a
mile. When they arrive, the soldiers lay Jesus on the ground, nail
his outstretched arms to the cross beam, then raise and attach it
to a post. A road runs alongside Golgotha, entering the city through
a nearby gate. People going in and out of the city have a good view
of Jesus. But any passerby with sympathy for a fellow creature in
agony does not look very long. Those condemned to crucifixion are
usually stripped naked (notice that the soldiers take Jesus' outer
and inner clothes), and Jesus has been scourged, an act that leaves
the victim's flesh in shreds.

A handful of Jesus' family and friends keep watch. His
mother is among them. That she steels herself to endure the sight
of her crucified son is testimony to her determination to be with
him in his suffering. "She stood there dying, without being able to
die," St. Bernard of Clairvaux remarked. Artists have depicted Mary
collapsing under the strain and needing her companions to support her.

Suffering with Her Son

At Cana, Jesus spoke to his mother about his "hour," meaning the
hour of his death. His words, then, were a gentle reminder that
he was proceeding on an agenda known fully to the Father and
the Son alone. The scene at Golgotha drives this point home with
heartbreaking force. How unfathomable even to Mary is Jesus' bond
of love with his Father that has led him to this suffering.

Yet the paradox of Cana continues at Golgotha. As a
created person, Mary stands outside the mystery of the eternal
Son's relationship with the Father, yet as his mother, she has
unique access to his mind and heart. At the wedding, she intuited
his intentions. She can hardly be less attuned to him now. Her
capacity to understand her son is limited; but can there be any
limit to her capacity to suffer with him? The bishops at the Second
Vatican Council wrote that Mary "faithfully persevered in her union
with her Son unto the cross. There she stood, in keeping with the

83

divine plan, enduring with her only begotten Son the intensity of his suffering, joining herself with his sacrifice in her mother's heart, and lovingly consenting to the immolation of this victim, born of her" (*Dogmatic Constitution on the Church*, 58).

Providing for His Mother

John 19:26–27. From the cross, Jesus sees his mother and "the disciple whom he loved." It is this disciple's testimony that forms the basis of the Gospel (see John 19:26, 35). With his dying breath, Jesus entrusts his mother to this disciple's care. Jesus and Mary have male relatives who would be first in line to take on this responsibility. But none of them believes in Jesus (John 7:3–7). It is fitting that Mary, the first to believe in him, should be in the care of a disciple.

This disciple will assume Jesus' care for Mary as her adult son. In turn, in whatever way she can, she will care for the disciple as a mother. The New Testament scholar R. Alan Culpepper comments that, by giving them to each other, Jesus carries out what the evangelist said of him at the Last Supper: "Having loved his own who were in the world, he loved them to the end" (John 13:1).

No doubt Jesus had earlier opportunities to make arrangements for his mother. By waiting until his dying moments, he indicates that his action has some deep meaning—a point that John underlines by telling us that it brought Jesus' mission to completion. What does it mean?

"Here is your son. . . . Here is your mother": with these words, Jesus gives the two most beloved people in his life a family relationship with each other. In this way, he reveals the meaning of the death he is undergoing. By the cross, Jesus is creating the family of those who receive him and share his life with the Father. It is only after his death—because it is *through* his death—that Jesus will be able speak of his disciples as "my brothers" and of God as *their* Father (John 20:17). By his death and resurrection Jesus makes them—and us—a new family in himself.

No woman has a deeper faith in Jesus than his mother, no man a deeper experience of Jesus' love than this disciple, who is never named in the Gospel but is referred to simply as the one "whom he loved." As mother, Mary brought Jesus into the world; as witness, this beloved disciple will bring testimony to Jesus out to the world. Thus, together Mary and this disciple exemplify the Church—the community of men and women who receive Jesus with total openness and make him known to everyone who believe in him and abide in his love. The night before his death, Jesus prayed for his disciples: "Holy Father, protect them in your name that you have given me, so that they may be one, as we are one" (John 17:11). As his mother and his closest friend leave Golgotha together, Jesus' prayer begins to be fulfilled.

Giving His Life

John 19:28–30. In his dying moments, the one who had turned water into wine is tormented by thirst. A soldier moistens his lips with a little wine from his own jug. Yet even in this extremity of suffering, Jesus is not a passive victim. He has allowed himself to be brought to this hour. In the end, his life is not taken from him; he willingly relinquishes it. With a deliberate bowing of his head, he hands over his spirit, giving his life to his Father as the sacrifice that removes sins. This opens the way for his disciples to receive his life. On the evening of his resurrection he will breathe on them, saying, "Receive the Holy Spirit" (John 20:22).

Reflections on the Reading

At Cana, Jesus indicated to his mother that her concern was not his concern, that he had to be guided by God's plan for him rather than anyone else's desires. "My hour has not yet come," he told her. At Golgotha, his hour has come, and perhaps surprisingly, it is revealed that the Father's plan includes Jesus' mother. At Cana, Jesus put a distance between his mother and himself, but at Golgotha he reaches out to her even in his suffering. He looks at her from the cross, speaks to her, and gives her a profound part to play in the community of his disciples.

Questions for Reflection and Discussion

45 minutes
Choose questions according to your interest and time.

1 Why do you think the chief priests objected to the placard on the cross (verses 19–21)?

2 Obviously, Pilate did not think Jesus was the king of the Jews. Why, then, did he insist on keeping the placard as written (verse 22)?

3 The one who could transform water into wine died in thirst, with only a sip of wine from one of his executioners to comfort him (verses 28–29). What does this suggest about the kind of person Jesus is and the kind of mission he came to carry out?

4 The early Church Father Origen said that Mary's faith was stretched to the limit at the cross. When has your faith in God's greatness and goodness been challenged by the presence of evil or suffering in the world? How have you responded to this challenge? Is Mary a helpful model and companion in those situations?

5 Jesus gave his life to create a community of men and women, each of whom is his beloved disciple. Might you relate to fellow Church members differently if you thought of each of them as Jesus' beloved disciple?

6 By giving his mother into the care of the beloved disciple, Jesus also placed the disciple in Mary's motherly care. How have you discovered Mary's motherly care for you?

7 Are there helpful and unhelpful ways of being with someone who is suffering? What lessons have you learned about this, from your experience of suffering and your experience of being with others in pain?

8 Imagine Jesus calling you the beloved disciple. What is your reaction? Why do you react as you do?

9 **Focus question.** Have you gotten a clearer picture of Mary from the Gospel readings and discussions of the past few weeks? What insight or discovery has been most meaningful for you? How will your life be different as a result?

Prayer to Close

10 minutes
Use this approach—or create your own!

♦ Pray the Hail, Holy Queen—a prayer that developed in the Middle Ages that is especially appropriate after meditating on Mary's presence at the cross. Pause for silent reflection and spontaneous prayers of any kind. End with an Our Father, a Hail Mary, and a Glory Be.

Hail, holy Queen, mother of
   mercy,
our life, our sweetness, and our
   hope.
To you do we cry, poor banished
   children of Eve,
to you do we send up our sighs,
mourning and weeping in this
   valley of tears.
Turn, then, most gracious
   advocate,
your eyes of mercy toward us,
and after this our exile
show unto us the blessed fruit of
   your womb,
Jesus.

O clement, O loving, O sweet
   Virgin Mary.

Living Tradition

Raised into Glory

Mary after the Crucifixion

Artists' depictions of the taking down of Jesus' body from the cross usually include Mary. But John's Gospel—the only one to mention her presence at the cross—is silent on this matter. Did she wait at Golgotha until his body was removed? Or had she reached the limits of endurance and needed to be escorted away? We can only speculate.

Jesus died on a Friday. On the following Sunday morning, some of his women disciples found his tomb empty. Then he appeared, alive, to them and, after that, to his male disciples. Did Jesus appear to his mother? There is no report of such an encounter in the New Testament. But the Gospels tell us that he appeared individually to Mary Magdalene and to Peter (John 20:11–17; Luke 24:34), and St. Paul informs us that he appeared separately to James, one of Jesus' male relatives (1 Corinthians 15:7). We are left to draw our own conclusion. The Byzantine tradition celebrates a meeting between the risen Jesus and his mother. A liturgical song cries out: "You despoiled Hades without a challenge. You, the giver of Life, met the Virgin. O Lord, risen from the dead, glory to you!"

Mary at Pentecost

We catch sight of Mary again in the Acts of the Apostles, St. Luke's narrative of the early Church. Mary is with the disciples on the Jewish feast of Pentecost as they gather in prayer, waiting for the Holy Spirit to come to them. Luke tells us that the male disciples "were constantly devoting themselves to prayer, together with certain women, including Mary the mother of Jesus" (Acts 1:14). Mary knew better than anyone what it means to be open to the Holy Spirit. As they prayed and waited for the Spirit, what could have been more encouraging to the disciples than Mary's presence?

Luke writes: "including Mary the mother of Jesus, as well as his brothers" (Acts 1:14). The brothers were there! They did not believe in Jesus during his ministry. But to one of them, at least, James, Jesus appeared after his resurrection (1 Corinthians 15:7). James's testimony probably had an effect on other men in the family. Thus, Mary found some healing of the pain she had felt when members of the family took a stand against her son. She must have been very happy for them.

After Jesus' Ascension

After Pentecost, Luke says nothing more about Mary. Apparently he wants to leave us with the picture of her among the disciples at Pentecost. John recounted how Jesus gave his mother to the beloved disciple, and thus to all of us who follow Jesus. Luke makes the same point with his final verbal icon of Mary sitting with the disciples as they pray. The image captures a lasting reality: Mary continues to be among Jesus' disciples, encouraging us to trust him, to obey him, to be open to the Holy Spirit.

Other New Testament writers say nothing more about Mary, and concerning the remainder of her earthly life we have no certain information. According to one tradition, she went with the beloved disciple to Ephesus, in present-day Turkey. A house said to be hers, a few miles outside the ruins of Ephesus, is shown to pilgrims. Another tradition maintains that she stayed in Jerusalem.

In Mary's time, elderly Jews living outside Palestine might retire to Jerusalem so that they could worship in the temple during their golden years. If Mary stayed on in Jerusalem, rather than returning to Nazareth, she followed this custom but for a different reason—not primarily to participate in worship at the temple but to be part of the Christian community, the temple of living stones that Jesus brought into existence through his death and resurrection. In addition, she would be close to the places where he had made the ultimate sacrifice and had conquered all the powers of evil.

The Assumption of Mary

Mystery surrounds the end of Mary's life in this world. Early generations of Christians were silent on the matter. But by the fifth century, the conviction had developed that Mary's body did not remain in this world. Rather, God raised her up into eternal life, allowing her already to experience resurrection in union with her son. She was assumed, or taken up, into heaven.

For a long time, Christians East and West held this belief and celebrated it in the liturgy without having a formal, dogmatic statement on the subject. But in the twentieth century, Pope Pius XII, after consulting Catholic bishops around the world, deemed it appropriate to make a clear declaration about Mary's assumption into heaven. "When the course of her earthly life was finished," he solemnly declared, "she was taken up body and soul into heavenly glory, and exalted by the Lord as Queen over all things, so that she might be the more fully conformed to her Son, the Lord of lords and conqueror of sin and death."

According to one tradition, Mary died before being taken into heaven. According to another tradition, she did not die, but God took her at the end of her life. Pius deliberately refrained from settling this issue. "When the course of her earthly life was finished" does not affirm or deny that Mary died; it leaves the question open.

Like her preservation from original sin from the first moment of her existence, Mary's assumption was a pure gift from God, an expression of grace to his "favored one." And just as her preservation from original sin through Jesus' death and resurrection is a sign of the purification that God wants to accomplish in our lives through Jesus, her assumption is also a sign of hope for us— an indication of what God has in store for us.

Calling Mary "queen" of heaven, as Pius did, highlights her sharing in her son's conquest of death. And it reminds us that Jesus calls each of us to experience victory over death with him. In the heavenly Jerusalem, "They need no light of lamp or sun, for the Lord God will be their light, and they will reign forever and ever" (Revelation 22:5).

Suggestions for Bible Discussion Groups

A Bible discussion group works best if you agree on where you're going and how you intend to get there. Many groups use their first meeting to talk over such questions. Here is a checklist of issues, with bits of advice from people who have experience in Bible discussions. (A discussion will go more smoothly if the leaders have thought through the following issues beforehand.)

Agree on your purpose. Are you getting together to gain wisdom and direction for your lives? To finally get acquainted with the Bible? To support one another in following Christ? To encourage those who are exploring—or reexploring—the Church? For other reasons?

Agree on attitudes. For example: "We're all beginners here," "We're here to help one another understand and respond to God's word," "We're not here to offer counseling or direction to one another," or "We want to read Scripture prayerfully." What do *you* wish to emphasize? Make it explicit!

Agree on ground rules. Barbara J. Fleischer, in her useful book *Facilitating for Growth*, recommends that a group clearly state its approach to the following:

- *Preparation.* Do we agree to read the material and prepare answers to the questions before each meeting?
- *Attendance.* What kind of priority will we give to our meetings?
- *Self-revelation.* Are we willing to help the others in the group gradually get to know us—our weaknesses as well as our strengths, our needs as well as our gifts?
- *Listening.* Will we commit ourselves to listen to one another?
- *Confidentiality.* Will we keep everything that is shared *with* the group *in* the group?
- *Discretion.* Will we refrain from sharing about the faults and sins of people who are not in the group?
- *Encouragement and support.* Will we give as well as receive?
- *Participation.* Will we give each person the time and opportunity to make a contribution?

You might take a pen and draw a circle around *listening* and *confidentiality*. Those two points are especially important.

The following items could be added to Fleischer's list:

◆ *Relationship with parish.* Is our group part of the adult faith-formation program? Independent but operating with the express approval of the pastor? Not a parish-based group?

◆ *New members.* Will we let new members join us once we have begun the six weeks of discussions?

Agree on housekeeping.

◆ *When will we meet?*

◆ *How often will we meet?* Meeting weekly or every other week is best if you can manage it. William Riley remarks, "Meetings once a month are too distant from each other for the threads of the last session not to be lost" (*The Bible Study Group: An Owner's Manual*).

◆ *How long will each meeting run?*

◆ *Where will we meet?*

◆ *Is any setup needed?* Christine Dodd writes that "the problem with meeting in a place like a church hall is that it can be very soul-destroying," given the cold, impersonal feel of many church facilities. If you have to meet in a church facility, Dodd recommends doing something to make the area homey (*Making Scripture Work*).

◆ *Who will host the meetings?* Leaders and hosts are not necessarily the same people.

◆ *Will we have refreshments?* Who will provide them? Don Cousins and Judson Poling make this recommendation: "Serve refreshments if you like, but save snacks and other foods for the end of the meeting to minimize distractions" (*Leader's Guide 1*).

◆ *What about child care?* Most experienced leaders of Bible discussion groups discourage bringing infants or other children to adult Bible discussions.

Agree on leadership. You need someone to facilitate—to keep the discussion on track, to see that everyone has a chance to speak, to help the group stay on schedule. Rena Duff, editor of the newsletter *Sharing God's Word Today*, recommends having two or three people take turns leading the discussions.

It's OK if the leader is not an expert on the Bible. You have this Six Weeks book as a guide, and if questions come up that no one can answer, you can delegate a participant to do a little research between meetings. Perhaps your parish priest or someone on the pastoral staff of your parish could offer advice. Or help may be available from your diocesan catechetical office or a local Catholic college or seminary.

It's important for the leader to set an example of listening, to draw out the quieter members (and occasionally restrain the more vocal ones), to move the group on when it gets stuck, to get the group back on track when the discussion moves away from the topic, and to restate and summarize what the group is learning. Sometimes the leader needs to remind the members of their agreements. An effective group leader is enthusiastic about the topic and the discussions and sets an example of learning from others and of using resources for growing in understanding.

As a discussion group matures, other members of the group will increasingly share in doing all these things on their own initiative.

Bible discussion is an opportunity to experience the fulfillment of Jesus' promise "Where two or three are gathered in my name, I am there among them" (Matthew 18:20). Put your discussion group in Jesus' hands. Pray for the guidance of the Spirit. And have a great time exploring God's word together!

Y ou can use this book just as well for individual study as for group discussion. Although discussing the Bible with other people can be a rich experience, there are advantages to reading on your own. For example:

◆ You can focus on the points that interest you most.
◆ You can go at your own pace.
◆ You can be completely relaxed and unashamedly honest in your answers to all the questions, since you don't have to share them with anyone!

My suggestions for using this book on your own are these:

◆ Don't skip "Questions to Begin" or "First Impression."
◆ Take your time on "Questions for Reflection and Discussion." A group will probably not have enough time to work on all the questions, but you can allow yourself the time to consider all of them if you are using the book by yourself.
◆ After reading "Exploring the Theme," go back and reread the Scripture text before moving on to "Questions for Reflection and Discussion."
◆ Take the time to look up all the parenthetical Scripture references.
◆ Read additional sections of Scripture related to the excerpts in this book. For example, read the portions of Scripture that come before and after the sections that form the readings in this guide. You will understand the readings better by viewing them in their context.
◆ Because you control the pace, give yourself plenty of opportunities to reflect on the meaning of the Scripture passages for you. Let your reading be an opportunity for these words to become God's words to you.

Bibles

The following editions of the Bible contain the full set of biblical books recognized by the Catholic Church, along with a great deal of useful explanatory material:

- ◆ *The Catholic Study Bible* (Oxford University Press), which uses the text of the *New American Bible*
- ◆ *The Catholic Bible: Personal Study Edition* (Oxford University Press), which also uses the text of the *New American Bible*
- ◆ *The New Jerusalem Bible*, the regular (not the reader's) edition (Doubleday)

Books, Web Sites, and Other Resources

- ◆ *Catechism of the Catholic Church.* Search under "Mary" in the index at the back of the *Catechism.*
- ◆ For prayers to Mary, see the Web site Prayers from Gregory the Wonderworker to Mother Teresa, at the University of Dayton: http://campus.udayton.edu/mary/prayers/SaintsPrayers.htm.
- ◆ Cardinal Carlo Maria Martini, S.J., *The Gospel Way of Mary: The Journey of Trust and Surrender.* Frederick, MD: The Word among Us Press, 2011.
- ◆ Cardinal James Hickey, *Mary at the Foot of the Cross: A Retreat Given to John Paul II and the Papal Household.* San Francisco: Ignatius Press, 1988.

How has Scripture had an impact on your life? Was this book helpful to you in your study of the Bible? Please send comments, suggestions, and personal experiences to Kevin Perrotta, General Editor, Trade Editorial Department, Loyola Press, 3441 N. Ashland Ave., Chicago, IL 60657.